Praise from Readers

"Joyce's experiences capture the essence of the NDE and expand on our knowledge of the devastating effects of suicide. The book is must reading for anyone hurting from life's experiences."
—Arvin S. Gibson, author, *Echoes from Eternity, Glimpses of Eternity,* and *Journeys Beyond Life*

"Joyce's willingness to share her remarkable experience and what she has learned shows her sincere desire to help others. Her message will be extremely valuable to all who are burdened by earthly challenges. There is power and wisdom in her candid personal sharing."
—Dr. Blaine Lee, vice president and founding owner, Covey Leadership Center

"*Heavenly Answers* . . . is compelling, liberating, and motivating. After reading it, every day looks brighter and is filled with more hope and love than before. Everyone would benefit from reading this book, especially those who think life isn't worth living."
—Gary and Joy Lundberg, authors, *I Don't Have to Make Everything All Better*

Continued . . .

"I want to thank Joyce Brown for putting things back in perspective for me. . . . It's great to be reminded in such a compelling way about what really matters most—now and in eternity."
—Janice Kapp Perry, author, composer

"This is a wonderful book—written from the heart. I could not put it down until I finished it and the next day I read it again. It offers uplifting coping techniques for living now and gives a glimpse of the Other Side with Joyce's premise throughout the book that *life is not a dress rehearsal*."
—Robert Frome, business owner, retired Lt. Col. U.S.A.F., former state assistant attorney general

"Normally I skim reading material. I found it impossible to do so with *Heavenly Answers* . . . , often rereading it for its special messages. This book is intelligently written, profoundly informative, and a rare gift."—Pat Graves, Fiber-Optic Communications

"The message from this book is profoundly significant. Joyce is truly fulfilling her mission to 'spread the word.' "   —Patrick Wayne Mumford, attorney-at-law

"Of the multitude of books that are written, every once in a while a book comes along that is a 'must read.' This is such a book."   —James Black, Ph.D.

"This book is a gift to anyone who is laboring in the dark shadows of depression, bringing them out into the light of His love."
—RaNelle Wallace, author of *The Burning Within*

"Joyce's vivid, candid account of her experience gives new understanding and meaning to the magnificence of the small things. After reading her book, I feel empowered."   —Carolyn Taylor, Ph.D.

"Thank you for writing your book. It gave me a different perspective about life and my problems. Now I have found reasons why I want to live instead of automatically wishing I could die or wanting to trade places with someone else."
                    —Michelle L., student, age 14

"This book is absolutely wonderful. Once I started reading, I could hardly put it down—everyone could benefit by reading it. What a beautiful message of hope for now and for the future!"
—Lee Saunders, master art conservator

"I have often thought of my children as work. After reading this book, I looked, really looked, at each of them and I saw them differently—they took my breath away. I loved this book. It has changed my life."   —Sheri Becar, mother of eight

"For years, I have held feelings against someone who was extremely unfair to me when I was ill and could not protect myself. A big burden lifted from me when I read this book and realized the person has not really gotten away with his actions—he has not robbed justice. This book has helped me in many ways."
                    —Barbara Browning, real estate and
                        mortgage loans

"This book is needed to make it through life's journey, to understand what really counts. It will be an excellent gift for people that I want to be sure know of needed heavenly answers for their earthly challenges."
                    —Gloria Bennett, hairstylist, barber

"This book truly opened my eyes to a realm I never thought existed before. I know I am a better person for having read it—it has the power to bless people's lives in extraordinary ways."
—Tracy Taylor, public relations

"This book has become the cornerstone of my life. I am using it as a guide for my future."
—Katylyn Reborio, age 15, high school student

"Joyce's shared revelations give personal strength to continue life with more positive insights."
—Shirley Frederickson, retired

"Initially I started reading my friend's copy of *Heavenly Answers* . . . and I was unable to put it down. Also, coping with day-to-day challenges is not always easy. I am so glad to have a source to refer to (and I will) for many of the answers."
—Sylvia Newton-Robbins, university director, seminar leader

"Joyce's story is moving, emotional, and takes you along with it. This is one of those rare books that can create new goals about living on earth in such a way as to enjoy heaven when getting there. This book can make a real difference in the world."
—June Davidson, president, American Seminar Leaders Association

"This book changed my whole life for the better."
—Kare Neve, businesswoman and mother of five

"Anyone even remotely considering suicide MUST read this book!"   —Cordell E. Logan, Ph.D., N.D.

HEAVENLY ANSWERS TO EARTHLY QUESTIONS

Simple Lessons for a Life Worth Living

Joyce H. Brown

Foreword by
Kimberly Clark Sharp, M.S.W.

A SIGNET VISIONS BOOK

SIGNET
Published by New American Library, a division of
Penguin Putnam Inc., 375 Hudson Street,
New York, New York 10014, U.S.A.
Penguin Books Ltd, 27 Wrights Lane,
London W8 5TZ, England
Penguin Books Australia Ltd, Ringwood,
Victoria, Australia
Penguin Books Canada Ltd, 10 Alcorn Avenue,
Toronto, Ontario, Canada M4V 3B2
Penguin Books (N.Z.) Ltd, 182–190 Wairau Road,
Auckland 10, New Zealand

Penguin Books Ltd, Registered Offices:
Harmondsworth, Middlesex, England

Published by Signet, an imprint of New American Library,
a division of Penguin Putnam Inc.

First Printing, January 2000
10 9 8 7 6 5 4 3 2 1

Lovingly dedicated:

To my family, friends, and associates who have encouraged me, cried with me, laughed with me, and endured my times of learning. My family had many hardships and pain of their own when I was ill and couldn't be with them. That, I wish I could change, but we have learned a lot, grown wiser, loved, and laughed. And, we have the promise of great tomorrows.

- To anyone along the way I may have offended as I was growing wiser and learning . . . I apologize.
- To all those who believed in me and cheered me on when things seemed darkest.
- To all those who have succeeded in life, leaving an easier path for others—including me—to follow.
- To all those who have entrusted me to be their mental cheerleader.
- To my ancestors and posterity, my Other Side's cheerleaders.
- To all those who have a desire to know more of the Other Side, to live life to its fullest, to not only find a better way, but to help create a better way of living and learning from and with each other.
- To those who endure and REAP LASTING PEACE OF MIND!

Acknowledgments

First, I want to sincerely thank the great Creator of us all for permitting me to have a second chance at life after my near-death experience.

I express love, gratitude, and appreciation to all those who encouraged me and so willingly helped me to make this book a reality.

Several months after my experience on the Other Side in 1983, I met and married Earl Brown. I sincerely thank and acknowledge his loving enthusiasm for this book, and for his encouragement and support, which continue beyond the day of his accidental death in 1998.

When my manuscript was first published and read by my family, a new closeness developed amongst us. Their continued and added encouragement for this book has been heartwarming. Not all can be named, but it is important to me that I acknowledge particular family members: my mother, and my three children, Suzan, Patty, and David, whose personal input and encouragement were very helpful; Shirley, Barbara, Crystal, Tara, Jen; Jim, Matthew, Lorina, Ki; and other special family and friends along the way.

Acknowledgments

Warren Jamison, agent, journalist, and author of several top-selling books. His enthusiasm for this project, his input, and help as I was preparing the manuscript for publication were immeasurable and invaluable. Gary and Joy Lundberg, authors of *I Don't Have to Make Everything All Better*, whose willingness to share their knowledge and give guidance has been priceless. RaNelle Wallace, author of *The Burning Within*, has given loving encouragement. Arvin Gibson, author of several books of people's experiences on the Other Side, including *Echoes from Eternity*, *Glimpses from Eternity*, has given valuable critiques and other great help. Gloria Bennett continually encouraged me to get the book written and published since 1983. Nancy Jackson, who, after reading my manuscript, had a life-changing experience, became devoted to sharing its message, and after the death of my husband, helped me in many ways.

Burt Chamberlain, Ed.D., M.S.W., whose interest and encouragement helped me to start writing. Lee and Joyce Saunders, master art conservator, sculptor, and friends who helped me keep writing. Carolyn Taylor, Ph.D., seminar leader, associate, and more, whose time and input have been very helpful. Carolyn Reborio, typist and friend, loyally typing, and typing . . .

we went through reams and reams of paper while I was finding and changing the words for this manuscript. Robert Davis, for his creative abilities, and for his patience in putting up with my innumerable changes in cover and text. And a special acknowledgment to Darla Hanks Isackson, whose editing help, insight, and inspired suggestions have been priceless.

Special, special thanks to Ken Atchity of AEI, my agent, and to Laura Anne Gilman, executive editor of New American Library, who did the final editing and condensing for this edition, yet still left my own words and the main message from my heart to my readers intact.

I would also like to thank the readers who have brightened many of my days when they wrote to me with their comments and stories of life-changing effects for them and their families. I especially want to thank over a hundred people who have told me they have changed their minds about committing suicide after reading *Heavenly Answers*. When I heard from my readers, it was like receiving a gift that helps me "keep on keeping on" with life's journey.

There are many others I want to thank who were part of my story, and encouraged me along the way, who are not mentioned in this book—I love and appreciate these friends and family, too.

FOREWORD

Kimberly Clark Sharp, M.S.W.,
author of *After the Light*

For anyone who has ever toyed with the notion of "ending it all" in an attempt to go
to the place of love and light, Joyce Brown offers
an important reality check. There is a reason
why we are here and why our life is not over,
no matter how bleak our current situation may
be. Immense rewards—spiritual rewards—await
those of us who persevere in the face of trials
and try our best to learn and to grow.

In my own book, I wrote: "The Light was
brighter than hundreds of suns but did not hurt
my eyes. I immediately understood it was entirely composed of love, all directed at me. I was
with my Creator, God, in holy communication.

The Light gave me knowledge that I seemed to be remembering rather than learning, and included answers to questions that any fool would ask in the presence of the Almighty. 'Why are we here?' To learn. 'What's the purpose of our life?' To love. And, among other questions, 'What about suicide?' The answer I understood was, 'If you didn't create it, you can't destroy it.' I took that as advice to not deliberately end our earthly lives prematurely. Why not? Well, if life is a metaphor for school, consider that if we drop out in, say, March, we cannot, at such time as we figure out we need more education, begin again in March. We have to repeat the entire school year and probably have to take remedial classes. We end up working harder than if we had stuck it out in the first place."

I wish I had been able to convince Joyce Brown of this earlier in her life, but then she would have missed the most remarkable experience of her life.

After a prolonged and serious illness with debilitating pain, Joyce Brown willed herself dead. She had a near-death experience, but it was not what she expected. Instead of bliss and blessedness, she had an "extremely anguishing experience" wherein she suddenly realized all that she had lost by giving up on life. The wispy spiritual body she now possessed could not speak to her loved ones or pick up pen and paper to write them. She was overwhelmed by a desperate longing for her pain-racked earthly body as she realized that she could no longer communicate to her family how much she loved and missed them. She had had her chance at earthly life and now it was over.

But fortunately for us, it wasn't over. A "beautiful Being of Light" ushered her into His presence and began to teach her about life. She saw that life is like a race and that it is important to continue that race until its natural end. The barriers and obstacles that we encounter along the way are there to help us learn and grow.

She was shown the agonies of people who had ended their lives early and who then tried desperately and without success to warn others who were present at their funerals. She came to know that there is no such thing as "ending it all" and that the problems people face may even get worse when they terminate their lives before their time.

She learned how people who appear to "have it all" really don't and why we would not want to trade places with those who seem to float through life unscathed by problems. She was taught why we have the problems we do and how we can learn from every situation, no matter how difficult.

Then she saw that rich rewards and priceless joys await many of the most humble people on earth who valiantly suffer through their trials and tribulations. Fortunately for whiners such as myself, complaining while suffering is okay.

She witnessed intense marital arguments from inside the mind of the participants and could see that what they were saying did not correspond to how they were really feeling. She saw the utter futility of bitter, heated disputes and learned how such conflicts could be resolved. She also saw a miserable place for souls who died while still holding on to their spiteful grudges.

Accordingly, Joyce came to understand that any deed we do with unrighteous motivation or intention actually hurts us. On the other hand, forgiveness—whether requested or not, whether deserved or not—brings heavenly rewards beyond comprehension.

In summation, the things we say and do on earth can drain or build our character and spiritual strength with results that show up when we arrive on the Other Side. The way Joyce figures it, we are literally building a heavenly retirement fund!

When confronted with the question "In life, what did you do with what you had?" none of the carefully crafted excuses that had previously shielded Joyce from accepting responsibility for who she was and how she acted had any effect. In re-experiencing everything that happened in her life, she realized that we "score" simply by how well we do with what we have.

She learned that miracles are actually common and happen more easily for those who believe in them. She was surprised that more of her prayers had been answered than she realized and that she had been blessed many times without knowing it. She also saw the difference in how beauty is created and valued on earth and how beauty is created and valued on the Other Side. Her insights reinforce the timeless truths from Jesus' Sermon on the Mount.

Joyce Brown asks us to please hear her message: Life Is Worth Living! I agree with my whole heart. There is a peace in knowing that a great leveling is coming, that every valley shall be exalted and every mountain and hill made low, that people who lead lives of challenge and heartache have greater growth opportunities than those who have lives of ease, that this is our chance to learn and grow spiritually, to experience and accomplish things that can take place only in an earthly existence.

We get up from reading this book grateful to be alive and to have the chance afforded by each day to do good and to be good. There is power in the lessons of this book, power that the least of us can use in meeting the challenges that come to us every day.

This book is about life and afterlife. It helps us understand the big picture—why we are here and why life unfolds as it does—and it helps us gain strength for the daily challenges we all face as long as we exist in earthly form. Life indeed is worth living and *Heavenly Answers to Earthly Questions* helps us understand our personal purpose and path.

PART ONE

❧

Anonymous and Comfortable

A few years ago, while deep in thought, I suddenly became aware of the midday news on television. The anchorman was discussing specific near-death experiences that people had related to him. Different experiences, but with one common theme: they were saying that it was so peaceful and beautiful on the Other Side that they hadn't wanted to come back.

Those descriptive words have no attraction for me. Instead, they now fill me with great remorse.

I wanted to cry out, "Please, you are telling how it is only for those who are ready to meet their Creator and who do not voluntarily take their own lives."

Silently staring at the television screen, I heard

a news item from a second reporter about two teens' suicides. A boy and a girl left a note saying that they had entered into a "love pact" before killing themselves. They did this mistakenly believing they would leave this earthly life to go to a more beautiful place where they would happily be together forever.

Earlier that week, a seventeen-year-old, who seemingly had everything to live for, had killed himself. He came from a well-respected family and was active in his religion and sports. He was admired in many ways and held a leadership position at school. From outward appearances he was truly living the American dream.

Many thoughts went through my mind as I heard the news commentator speculating on the cause of his suicide. Too much stress at school? Too much peer pressure? An investigation was in progress to determine whether the three dead teens had known each other. Were there connecting factors, or should their deaths be categorized as unexplained "chain suicides"?

As I listened to the newscaster stating possible reasons for those young people killing themselves, I shuddered. I was literally quivering as I went to the television set and answered it as if I could be heard. "No! No! Those are not the reasons those teens killed themselves." I felt I had to warn the newscasters of the dangers in unequivocally using phrases such as "how beautiful and peaceful it is on the Other Side."

· False Beliefs Can Lead to Tragedy

Falsely believing that in death they will find relief from all worldly cares can be a powerful enticement for those who feel overwhelmed enough to kill themselves—especially troubled young people. I know of such feelings from personal experience!

After the news broadcast was over, I sat on the couch wondering what I could do that might make a difference. Feeling compelled to speak up, to do something, I realized I could do it in a safe way, and I dialed the phone number for the television station.

A woman answered with the call letters of the station. My voice was trembling, but I expressed my feelings about the dangers of the words used by the newscaster. After a pause she said, "Just a moment, please," and put me on hold. I wanted to hang up, but the security of being distanced by the telephone, of being a nameless, faceless person just telling the station my opinion, gave me the courage to hold on.

The Other Side Is Not Always Nice

After a time, a man's voice came on the line. "Can I help you?" he asked. With a jolt I recognized the voice of the anchorman himself, the one who had reported the teen suicides. My nervousness began to disappear as I explained the possible danger in how teenagers and others could perceive his program's message.

"It's not always beautiful for someone on the Other Side," I went on in fervent tones. "The Other Side is not a place to escape problems. It is only peaceful over there if the timing is right and we do not give up on life. When someone gives up and commits suicide, they may discover on the Other Side that there were answers available for them on earth for their problems. This may cause them to feel tremendous anguish and it can be terrible for them over there."

His quick reply caught me totally off guard. "How do you know?" It seemed as if the telephone receiver was made of lead. I didn't feel like a nameless, faceless person anymore, but I also knew I had to answer his question truthfully. Up until this moment, I had shared my experiences on the Other Side only with those few I had felt comfortable telling about the matter. Now, all my previous reluctance to speak out felt like something tangible that surrounded me.

How Do I Know? I've Been There!

"Because I've been there," I answered with calm assurance. I felt as though I were standing in a public arena making my announcement to the whole world. If he asked me, I knew I would have to meet with him personally, speak up, answer his questions, and tell him what I had experienced. That would mean leaving my comfortable, anonymous position to substantiate the statements I had made. However, I was ready—even for interrogation if necessary.

My thoughts seemed to hang in the air as I waited for his response. . . . Silence! At last he asked for confirmation in a softer, more open tone, "You have been to the Other Side and back personally?"

When I assured him that I had, he continued, "What you experienced over there makes you believe that there's a connection between these teenage suicides and our television coverage of people's stories about how happy they were on the Other Side and how beautiful it was? Is that correct?"

"Yes. Most definitely, yes," I answered quickly. "Even if there's only a remote possibility that your broadcasts were a contributing cause and were glamorizing suicide, can you afford to take the chance?"

This time he didn't hesitate, but said in a friendly tone. "My co-anchor on the show has been concerned about this himself. We'll take the matter under advisement here at the station. Thank you for calling." With that he hung up.

Lasting Peace

Oh, what a relief! I was back to my comfortable, anonymous position even though I had not backed away from his questions. I had listened politely, and I felt I had accomplished something by communicating at least a tiny part of what I had experienced on the Other Side. One reason I had wanted to come back to this life was to warn others and to share how to find real joy and peace of mind over there . . . lasting peace.

It was Wednesday. Later that day I found out that the televised newscast that prompted my call was the third in what was to be a five-part series for the week, and each aired both morning and evening.

Self-Deluding "Love Pact"

The seventeen-year-old boy had killed himself within hours of the first evening's broadcast. The boy and girl who had made the "love-pact" had killed themselves within hours of the second evening's broadcast. This, the third, was scheduled to be rebroadcast on the evening news. Five more broadcasts were to come.

Fearing the effect the broadcasts could have, I wondered if what I had said could make any difference. Sitting down again on the couch, I leaned back, closed my eyes, and waited anxiously for the program to come on.

Finally, it was time. I was pleased to find that telling the news commentator some of my experiences from being on the Other Side had made a difference—the remaining broadcasts "glamorizing" the teens' chain suicides were canceled.

Why I Had to Write This Book

"Let me out of here . . . I want to die!" Those words expressed my feelings from the time I was a small child. If I had been asked whether I wanted to live or die, the truthful answer usually would have been, "I want to die."

From my youth, I remember hearing how nice it was on the Other Side and how happy people were after they died and left this earthly existence. Life after death sounded appealing to me, far more so than my life at the time.

However, in January 1983, when I was 49 years old, I had an experience that forever changed my view about committing suicide or even voluntarily giving up and choosing to die. It involved my own long-desired death—and a glimpse of the life beyond. Some people call such events near-death experiences, and they are talked about more openly now than in the past, for which I am grateful. This openness helped me have the courage to share my experience on the Other Side.

During my near-death experience I discovered that the imagination can falsely influence a person, causing him or her to think that killing oneself will take one to a better place than this world. It's true that a glorious, peaceful sphere may await us after we die. Suicide, however, will not put us there!

Now I see life, death, and life after life from a whole new perspective. Also, I know now that life is precious beyond all comprehension and that our time here is too precious to waste.

The Race of Life

While on the Other Side, I saw that life is similar to a race that starts at birth, and that when I was on earth I was one of the participants. I saw scenes of a race, and I was running with other runners along a designated course. Then thoughts came to my mind: what if somewhere in the course of the race, I decided I couldn't wait to get to the finish line? Maybe I was too tired to go on, or I felt the race was harder than I had anticipated. Would this justify my cutting across the field, running directly to the finish line, crossing it, then expecting to claim the rewards of a great victory?

What would I really have accomplished? Even if I might fool those who didn't see me cheat, did I think I could fool the judges? Did I think they might conveniently be looking away at the exact moment I took the shortcut? Or could I console myself with the wish that they loved me so much they would forgive me—that no consequences would flow from my fraudulent action?

Did I think I could be considered a winner if I didn't earn the victory? I knew it would be an empty victory—in reality, a defeat. Even if the judges forgave me, I would still know. How long would I carry my guilt and shame before I would be able to forgive myself? Lastly, what of the others who witnessed my cheating and were influenced also to take the shortcut? Would I not hold a part of their guilt as well? I recognized even at that moment that taking a shortcut in a race is symbolic of suicide.

No Competition

On the Other Side, I discovered that life is precious and that only if I explored it to its natural conclusion could I have the peace of mind and victory I hoped to claim. Also, knowledge was given me that during my time on earth I was not competing with anyone but myself. I knew that the only approval I really needed was from that Loving, All-Knowing Being, the Creator of the Universe—and from within myself.

My Father's Near-Death Experience

But before that, I was like those teenagers. I had heard accounts of individuals who have had near-death experiences and who tell of their wonderful feelings of peace. It so affects them that they are powerful witnesses to the beauty of the Other Side. Sometimes others who are troubled hear these stories and become convinced that they could find that love and peace—if only they could die. I believed that!

When I was in my teens, my father told me of the near-death experience he had had in the early 1950s when he was seriously injured in a car accident. He told me all he saw, which encouraged and reinforced my tendency to view death as an escape from my problems on earth rather than to seek solutions in this life.

The near-death experience that my father had, I believe, had a tremendous effect on him, too. Later, in July 1980, when life apparently seemed overwhelming to him, he committed suicide. I had not heard from him for some time before I received the phone call telling me of his death.

At the graveside services for my dad, I sat staring at his steel-gray coffin. The atmosphere felt dark and heavy to me. It was as if I could feel some of the despair he felt before he took his life. I foolishly thought about joining him in death, not realizing that suicide could lead me to anguish rather than peace.

My father's death by suicide is not something I have generally made known. The decision to mention it here follows deep soul-searching. The last thing I want to do is hurt those close to me—members of my family who did not know. Suicide is a subject usually not discussed. His suicide was sad, but it happened, and it added to my misguided idea that suicide was a positive alternative.

Because of What I Know, I Must Speak Up

Because of the fear that I might hurt someone's feelings, I was reluctant at first to speak up. I would not want to cause pain to anyone who has lost a loved one to suicide. Yet, I know that there are innumerable people who mistakenly feel as I did, when I believed that all I would have to do is give up and die or commit suicide to find lasting happiness. As with that television report, I feel compelled to share what I experienced and what I personally learned on the Other Side, in the hope that it will save lives and needless anguish for many.

When I was on the Other Side, I gained a new perspective from what I was shown and what I learned from glimpses of premortal life. Scenes of the spirit world, including revelations of knowledge, were impressed upon my consciousness. When viewed from the perspective of life in the hereafter, everything fits together perfectly. Because of what I learned there, the real purpose for living and making right decisions became clear—as did the reasons not to give up when tempted to do so.

A Whispering of the Spirit

Recently, I was very ill, and there were several days when I wondered if I would be called to the Other Side—this time for good. That thought greatly worried me; I did not want to die before I finished what I was supposed to do on earth. I knew that more was expected from me because of what I had been shown on the Other Side. I had not yet shared this experience with some special loved ones because I was worried about finding the right words and about what their reactions would be.

Being so ill, and completely losing my voice for more than two months, kindled my fear that I might never be able to share my experience. A soft whispering of the Spirit came to me with a question: "What is your priority now? If you could, would you speak up? Fear ye man more than God?" I came to the point that all I could think about was recording my experience. When my health returned, I began working on it immediately.

If I can help anyone realize the importance of living life in a way that can help achieve a portion of the joy and peace of mind available on the Other Side, I must do it. I want peace of mind the next time I die. When I am questioned again as to what I did with what I had, I hope I can say that I helped many others with the knowledge I was given.

PART TWO

❦

Heavenly Answers to Earthly Questions

Growing up in my home was difficult. I knew that my father hadn't wanted a baby unless it was a boy—which meant he didn't want me! He left my young mother before I was a year old, and I grew up feeling like a burden. I seldom saw my father, and I felt he had rejected me. I thought I was the cause of Mother's extreme financial difficulties and hated myself for being born. This added to my thinking that I could undo my life by ending it.

As a child I always heard that the Other Side was a beautiful and peaceful place. There was never any suggestion that you might not get to that place if your death was brought about by your own actions. I believed Heaven was such a beautiful and peaceful place that dying and going there would be better for me than living. From early childhood on, when I felt overwhelmed or depressed, I would mistakenly think, oh, well, I can choose to go to Heaven anytime. All I have to do is die to get there. Then I will be happy.

Does Just Thinking about Suicide Harm Us?

I don't remember how or when I first heard of a person taking his or her own life. But I distinctly remember thinking about suicide and actions I could take to kill myself when I was about eight years old.

Soon, suicidal thoughts became habitual whenever I was confronted with unhappy circumstances. Such thoughts short-circuited my thinking and my ability to find solutions for problems. When difficult things happened, I could always fall back to the comforting notion that I did not have to stay in this life and look for solutions. I believed the myth that I could choose to die and go to eternal happiness whenever I wished.

My school years were a maze of unhappiness. I was overweight and the brunt of painful teasing, taunting, and bullying, so I didn't like going to school. Because my mother worked long hours, when I was home I was alone, feeling rejected, bored, and depressed. I became argumentative as I grew older and misused my abundant energy in activities such as neighborhood rock fights.

The more miserable I became, the more frequently I thought of suicide. By the age of eighteen I was unhappily married, so shy and withdrawn it was stressful for me even to leave the house to get the mail or the newspaper. At twenty-four I was divorced and left to provide for my three children.

I prayed for relief and was guided to a unique self-improvement course utilizing sleep-teaching principles. I had not previously realized the importance of my thinking and how it influenced my behavior. By reinforcing my mind with positive thoughts, I truly created a new life and a new me.

But even though life for me on earth had become more enjoyable, I still had to face the trials that come to all of us every day, simply by virtue of being alive. Some were small, some were great, but they all caused me suffering. Nothing seemed as desirable as the peace and joy I mistakenly believed instantly available on the Other Side. To die as soon as possible instead of living and having to find solutions to my problems still sounded appealing.

Is There a Purpose in Illnesses and Trials?

When I was twenty-six I was injured in an automobile accident, which led to eight spinal surgeries during the next fifteen years. I suffered other health challenges as well and was never free of debilitating pain. Each time I had surgery I was almost helpless and was unable to care for my children for long periods of time. It broke my heart that my children grew to adulthood and married without the stability of the home life I yearned to provide for them.

In 1975 I had a massive spinal fusion that was supposed to help relieve some of the pressure on the nerves in my lower back. But the operation was unsuccessful. Something went wrong, and my condition rapidly worsened. As my muscles atrophied, my rebuilt life crumbled all around me. The diagnosis was that I would be left paralyzed, with excruciating pain, and would need to be sent to a nursing home to live out my life.

According to logic, reason, and medical science, I would never walk again. Gradually and miraculously, however, I forced, willed, and prayed movement back into my body and legs. I realized that the hardest times sometimes teach us the most. I experienced the reality of God's power in my life, and my determination grew. In a few weeks I made enough progress that I was released from the hospital and moved to a hospital bed in my living room.

My mother and my four-year-old granddaughter, who lived with us, worked tirelessly to care for me. My mom, in addition to her daily job, prepared our food, and my granddaughter would retrieve it from the refrigerator at mealtimes. She was loving and sweet, like a little angel, and she helped me in endless ways, both physically and emotionally.

During the time when I was confined to bed I meditated and studied books that opened my mind to future possibilities. Looking back, I see God's purpose unfolding in that opportunity too.

Eventually, with the help of back braces, leg braces, and an electrical unit to help block the pain, I walked on my own.

From my traumatic health problems and work experiences, I had learned the value of hope and of working for a worthwhile cause. I traveled, pursued further education, and came up with creative ideas for an environmental health business. My faith and my desire to succeed in the promising work opportunities kept me going. Being actively involved and continuing my education kept me from dwelling on my many physical problems and helped my mental well-being. As my knowledge increased, so did my confidence. I attended international business conferences and special seminars and learned of technologies that helped me develop a business that provided environmental solutions to private and government agencies. I hired a firm with people I thought were the best in this field to be my agents and manage the business. On the books, everything seemed to be going right, but my agents always seemed to have valid reasons to put off paying me my share of the profits. I was hopeful, but was being financially drained.

What Can Make a Person Want to Die?

In December 1981 I awakened late one night with a severe pain in my right eye. A dim night-light cast the only glow in my dark bedroom. As I was getting up to find out what was wrong with my eye, I found that my leg muscles wouldn't support me. In the near-darkness, I lost my balance and fell. My face struck something on the floor that fractured my skull in two places around my left eye socket. However, my attention was predominantly on the pain in my right eye. It felt as though a large foreign object of some kind was in it.

The next morning I went to an ophthalmologist. After examining my eye, the doctor put a patch over it, saying I had scratched the cornea. He said he would not know for ten days whether I would lose the vision in it. X rays showed the skull fractures.

Hardly believing this was happening to me, I nervously laughed when I looked in the mirror at myself with a swollen black eye on the left and a big patch on the right. It became even more of a struggle to be positive and to avoid feeling sorry for myself.

Later, I learned that these were some of my better days for a long time to come!

A bleak and lonely Christmas came and went while I was not only housebound with pain but worried that I might be losing my vision. On New Year's Eve, I was still confined to the house, sitting in my living room, feeling sad that I had missed all the fun of the holidays with my friends and family.

Feeling water dripping on me, I looked up and saw the ceiling over my head sagging. With a shock I realized that the roof was leaking. I had replaced the roof only three years before—an expensive, messy job I didn't want to go through all over again.

Everything seemed to be crashing in on me at once: my loneliness, the stress associated with my business and lack of money, the severe pain in my back, the possible loss of my vision, and now the leaking roof. I sat in the chair pondering the many problems that weighed on me while I watched the water fall on the furniture. My old habit of thinking resurfaced: "Oh, let me out of here! I want to die. I just want to die."

While I was still recovering in January 1982, I fell again. I went down hard and broke my tailbone. It hurt terribly. (Later, the muscle weakness that caused my falls was diagnosed as myasthenia gravis—muscular dystrophy.)

Respiratory infections began plaguing me, and I was bedridden with one illness after another. I would get a sore throat and be unable to get over it. The doctors weren't sure what to do as I began having severe reactions to the prescribed antibiotics. I began hurting and aching all over. My muscles were weak and I had trouble swallowing. "If I cannot get well," I thought again, "I just want to die."

As time passed, I became physically worse, with episodes of intense sweating followed by intense chills. Also, I developed an allergic reaction to the chemicals in my clothing. In fact, many items in my environment that had never bothered me before now would trigger a series of sweats that would leave me drenched, and then I would become chilled. My condition fluctuated, but I became progressively worse. The doctors couldn't tell me what was wrong without running extensive tests. Since I no longer had insurance, I could not afford the tests.

I began praying that I truly would die.

Is There a Choice to Live or Die?

As the pain became more severe, I began asking caring friends to pray with me that I could die and be released from these trials. They told me they were praying for God's will to be done. They also said that they felt that I was going through this for a purpose, but that I would have my choice to live or die.

I had made my choice. I wanted to die!

The bronchitis and respiratory infections continued. Then I began bleeding from up inside my head and down my throat. I would wake up in the mornings almost unable to breathe. I consulted an ear, nose, and throat specialist, but X rays showed no medical problems and the doctor could not pinpoint a cause for my problems.

A whole year had gone by since I started this downward spiral. It was December 1982, and I was still painfully alive. Believing that my family didn't need me anymore, I continued to pray for a natural death so I could be released from this living hell called life. The pain in my joints and body increased, and I could walk only by bracing myself on furniture.

Why Do Some People Just Seem to Give Up?

In January 1983, a doctor whom I greatly respected performed some tests that revealed I had a low white blood cell count, so I was not fighting off the infections; I would continue to get worse. Also, I was informed that the tests revealed I had rheumatoid arthritis; in a short period of time I would be in a wheelchair, never to walk again. Between the increasing pain and the worsening rheumatoid arthritis, and inability to fight the continued infections, I would most likely get pneumonia and die a natural death.

On the day I heard this news, I believed God was handing me my ticket to paradise. I wouldn't have to commit suicide, I thought. I would just die. I was happier than others would be if they had unexpectedly won tickets to Hawaii.

It was physically difficult that day to take my shower, but feeling so elated about dying gave me a little extra energy. I was fantastically happy that I was going to die and go to my imagined place of "forever happiness and joy." As the water sprayed over me, I was thinking of how wonderful I was going to feel when I left all my problems behind.

A song came to my mind and I sang parts of it joyfully: "Somewhere over the rainbow . . . where troubles melt like lemon drops, away above the chimney tops, that's where you'll find me." The words and melody of that tune stayed in my mind for hours and lulled me to sleep that night with pleasant thoughts of my coming "trip." Those words portrayed the new attitude I had for the next few days.

My dying, I thought, would take a little time, but that was okay! It meant I would be able to complete my earthly affairs, such as making my burial arrangements. I would have to take care of that slowly because I was so ill. Still, I wouldn't leave my family in chaos, and that was important to me. I believed it would be much better for my loved ones when I died.

What Is It Like to Die?

A few days later, I felt weaker and more ill than ever. I was alone that day. As the morning wore on, I continued to feel much worse. I began worrying. I thought, I can't die yet; I'm not quite ready.

I wanted to pray but was too weak to kneel on my own. The bathroom was large and attractive, with an ivory marbled tub and white lace shower curtains. I decided I would use the edge of the bathtub to lean on. I managed to get into the bathroom, even though the pain in my body was intense and I had lost most of my strength. Supporting myself by leaning over the side of the tub, I maintained as reverent a posture as I could to pray.

I wanted to pray for just enough strength to finish a few critical tasks before I died. I bowed my head in prayer, but before I was able to formally ask, I heard a voice as distinct and clear as if the speaker were standing directly above me. The voice said, powerfully, "If you come, you come now!"

With that, my strength left me and I slumped forward. All the air went out of me, and I felt a sinking heaviness in my body. With a swoosh up and outward, I left my body and found myself behind and slightly elevated from it, my feet not touching the floor. I felt weightless and the physical pain was gone.

I had thought that when people died, they went through a tunnel away from the world with its challenges and its problems to the beautiful, happy place I'd heard about—but I did not do that. I was shocked that dying was not what I had expected it to be. The room seemed to have no limitations to my view as I looked up, around, and then down. My attention focused on my body, slumped lifelessly over the tub.

Immediately, I noticed the difference between seeing myself from the mirror's flat surface and observing my body's shape as another person could see it, including a total view from the back. Looking around, I realized that my sight was not limited to the use of my eyes. I had always thought of vision as occurring in the one direction I focused on. But I could see behind me and in front, as well as above me. In this sphere, there was sort of an instant visual awareness of everything around me.

I felt wispy, almost transparent. I was aware that I could go through a wall and my hand could go through anything. I was also very aware of my limitations without my body; the knowledge was simply there. Anything I had not said while on earth would remain unsaid, anything I had not written while on the earth would not be written. I could not pick up anything—not even a piece of paper.

How Real Is the Spirit World?

It is difficult to describe what happened next. Events did not slowly progress from one phase to another as they had when I was alive on earth. Everything seemed to be happening almost instantaneously. Consequently, it is difficult to separate this experience into periods of time or to differentiate it into stages. The Other Side's dimension and my experiences there were a whole, like a hologram. God's universe was complete. It was magnificent beyond belief and absolutely beyond earthly description.

Vast knowledge and immeasurably deep feelings relating to my own personal development accompanied everything I experienced on the Other Side. This was the most vivid, personal experience I have ever known. I have struggled to find the right words to share this marvelous, yet extremely anguishing experience.

Vividly aware that I was in a spiritual realm, I knew I was in a sphere of afterlife, a place without my body, a space and time before resurrection. I had not realized that there were distinct phases of afterlife—the spirit world, when I would be without my body, and the resurrection, when my spirit and body would be reunited.

This different realm was more realistic, more authentic to me than the earth-life sphere. This was, without question, the most stark, real thing I had ever experienced; all else seemed insignificant in comparison. But I was shocked that nothing in the spirit world was as I had expected it to be.

Everything fit with a sharp reality, however. I had read in the Bible that the spirits of some people who had died long before Christ were finally reunited with their bodies after His Resurrection. I realized that they must have been in a wispy spirit world similar to this one until the time of their resurrection.

A desperate longing for my physical body overwhelmed me. Even though I had been terribly limited on earth because of ill health, I was drastically more limited without my body than I had been with it. I wanted to communicate with my family, to tell them I loved them and missed them, but I could not.

My chance on earth was over, and now it was too late. I realized with feelings of remorse that what I had thought of as dying and being in a state of "paradise" was not at all as I had anticipated.

Can We Have a Personal Relationship with the Creator?

Suddenly I was in the presence of a beautiful Being who radiated an overpoweringly brilliant white light. I knew that my natural eyes could not have endured this light. The Presence was brighter than anything I could have imagined. He was glorious and inspiring—radiant with love. I was filled with an awesome knowledge about God and His power.

How humbling! I felt I should bow or kneel to show my reverence. I had always loved my Creator, but I had never felt an actual personal relationship with Him.

Suddenly all of that changed.

Does God Love Us Unconditionally?

My love for God was greater than I had thought possible, beyond my earth life's comprehension. I realized that God loved me unconditionally and that He knew all about me. My own self-awareness of my thoughts and actions was sharply intensified. I wanted to shrink from the presence of this Being of Love and Truth. I felt great anguish, remorse, and sorrow for things I had done in life that I knew I should not have done, and for things I knew I ought to have done that I did not do while I was alive on earth.

As my understanding increased, my love for the Creator of the Universe increased. I felt an overwhelming appreciation for the blessings I had received in earth life. However, the more I realized the opportunities I had had in life, the more my anguish about not having used my time on earth better intensified.

The Personage standing before me radiated such a bright light that it was difficult to make out particular features. But He was powerful, all-knowing, and so loving. I felt His unconditional love radiating throughout my mind and soul. I had no idea there could be so much love for or from anyone, or that I had the ability to have these deep feelings of love for someone else. Instantly I knew that people do not have to be in a high-ranking position in earth life for God to love them. His love is boundless, limitless. He loves everyone, and I realized how important all of us are to Him.

I thought of loving someone with an intense and all-encompassing emotion, the most love anyone could ever feel for a child or a companion, and I knew that kind of love is nothing compared to the love we have for our Creator as we come to know Him.

What Was It Like to Be in the Presence of a Being of Light and Love?

My earlier thinking was that if I could have a moment with God, or someone representing Him, there would be many questions I would like to ask. But I discovered I didn't desire to ask Him anything. I just wanted to enjoy His presence, to bask in His love, to be with Him.

Then I thought about being reunited with loved ones after a long separation. I would want only to be in their presence, to love them, to feel their love for me in return. Bringing them up to date on events or quizzing them would seem foolish.

Feeling encircled in this love was a wondrous experience. I knew that the most horrible thing that could ever happen to me, my family, friends, or any of us who knew God would be to do something that would cut us off from His presence. To be anywhere else but in that presence would truly be hell.

Are There Answers Waiting for our Questions?

In the presence of this Personage of Light, I was instantly and keenly aware of the fact that God is real! Not merely an idea, or a theory, but a real person whose very presence pierced my soul. Instantly, a new understanding flooded my mind. Suddenly I was aware of a definite purpose to our earthly existence. At the same time, all the thoughts I'd had during my life came to the fore, and I began receiving heavenly answers for the questions I had always wanted to ask.

Are Communication and Learning Different on the Other Side?

With my newfound understanding of God's love, I also knew I had let Him down. As I realized this, my understanding was further opened. Knowledge flooded my consciousness, and thousands of different subjects instantaneously lit up my comprehension. This experience simply defies explanation.

It wasn't that this knowledge was coming from an outward source—it was as though knowledge that had always been within me was awakened. It was as if, in an instant, a cloud evaporated from my mind, and I had access to more knowledge and understanding than I had ever imagined. I call these understandings "eternal truths."

In the holy writings of almost all religions, many great truths are taught in symbolic parables; perhaps some of the things I was shown were visual parables of great truths. In this presence, I saw things I was familiar with used as representations of concepts. Words were not necessary, and thoughts were simply known, in a more pure and higher form of communication.

By comparison, earth-life communications seemed limiting and archaic. The free flow of ideas and instant understanding were so much quicker and clearer in the spirit realm. It was communication from mind to mind, being to being.

Can We Tune In to Eternal Truth While on This Earth?

Always-present knowledge, eternal truth that in some way constantly surrounds us, was revealed to me. I understood that many of these eternal truths are also available during earth life, although they are not easily perceived. They are available when the time is right and an individual is willing to make a deliberate effort to tune in to the right wavelength. I was filled with a stark reality of knowledge. I discovered there is no new truth. Truth is eternal and ever-present. We are simply so overwhelmed by our daily life on earth that we often cannot see it.

But now, suddenly, the answers to questions

and challenges I had in life came so quickly and seemed so obvious that I felt repentant for even wondering. I understood reasons for problems and answers to problems. I immediately yearned to come back to earth life and share what I had learned with my family, loved ones, and others.

Despite my bliss at being in this presence, I was equally aware that I had created an anguishing hell for myself, because I could have done more with my time on earth than I did. I knew that time, as it was known on earth, was limited, running out like sands in an hourglass beginning at birth and continuing until death. Time was to be used wisely and once spent, it could not be called back. Earth life was the foreign sphere, and time on earth was temporary, limited, and precious!

How Do Our Wrong Deeds and Attitudes Hurt Us as Well as Others?

Thinking of some of the people I had known in my life who had wasted a lot of their time hurting others, I realized that God sorrowed when they did wrong, but He still loved them. Feeling great sadness for them, I realized how they were really hurting themselves. I understood that each person has a definite purpose for living and only so much earth time to fulfill that purpose.

Viewing my own life's experiences, I saw that learning self-control is a great challenge and takes time. Some of the greatest strengths we can develop are those required to control feelings and emotions, especially the strength required to harness the tongue. However, I saw rich, eternal rewards, such as better family relationships, that could be reaped by striving to master these things.

I knew that every act of kindness carries a reward. It was amazing to me that even little kind acts could reap very large rewards. Every good attitude, everything right I had ever done in my physical body had been a gift to God and to me.

My new understanding included knowing that any wrong deed I had done with unrighteous motivation or intention was actually hurting me. Many rewards that could have been mine were lost because of my own actions or my sins of omission. I was shown how everything I did during my earth life had consequences; every action I took had a definite reaction and brought an appropriate reward or a just punishment—a cause and effect, as if I were planting seeds and eventually reaping exactly what I sowed.

With this understanding, scenes flashed quickly before my view and I saw farmers of all eras—weary, medieval peasants tilling the ground with crude stick tools, others dragging wooden plows, then futuristic, sophisticated machines crawling over immense fields, row after row, field after field, planting seeds. My interest was not on the farmers or their surroundings; I was fascinated with the seeds and the miracles of growth connected to them.

Time was compressed. No sooner had they planted than they began harvesting what they had sown. Those who planted corn reaped corn, those who planted carrots reaped carrots. Those who planted rice reaped rice. No one planted carrots and reaped apples. Whatever was planted was harvested—in its own kind.

Then the scenes changed. Now people were harvesting love and kindness because they had sown love and kindness with their actions. Beside them, others were reaping hateful, hurt feelings and violence because they had sown hate and hurting of others with their intent and actions.

Every kindness, every right decision, every forbearance was returned in kind; every cruel act, every hurtful decision, every quick-tempered retort reaped a like result. As these scenes were playing before my view, I recalled a proverb I had heard during earth life: As ye sow, so shall ye reap (Galatians 6:7).

Can We Escape Reaping What We Sow?

The messages of the scenes I viewed became clear to me: forgiveness yields forgiveness, mercy yields mercy, love yields love, violence yields violence—the harvest of anger at others is anger directed at oneself. The eternal truth is that we cannot escape harvesting what we plant.

Do We Choose Our Own Joy or Agony?

Then I knew that earth life is a time to plant, and the Other Side is the ultimate time of the law of the harvest—as we sow, so shall we reap. I was reaping anguish because of what I had sown during my earth life. I had made my own choices in life as to how to think and act. With my thoughts, actions, and reactions to situations and to others' actions I had created for myself what I was receiving. I had not realized that while I was alive on earth I had been building my character, my spiritual being, and determining my own harvest of eternal rewards, or lack thereof. I discovered that I chose joy or agony by my thoughts and actions during my earth life.

Also, I had a vivid awareness that studying Scriptures and holy writings would have revealed great truths that were grand keys to solving problems, achieving lasting peace of mind and eternal enjoyment.

During my earth life, my love and knowledge of the great Creator of the Universe was limited, but now I was filled with His love for me and mine for Him. My love and gratitude to Him for my many blessings seemed endless; my love for others was increased—it was all-encompassing—and I realized how important we all are to each other. Again, I was filled with anguish for not having used my time on earth more productively. I had wasted precious time wanting to die.

Being in the presence of this Personage of Love and Light made me wish I had used every minute I had on earth planting love so I could reap its blessings.

What Is the Harvest Reaped from Suicide?

Suddenly I seemed to be transported through time with scenes quickly passing my view. Then

I was in a chapel with flowers everywhere—large, beautiful bouquets on pedestals. The room was crowded with somber people; the only sounds were soft whispers and muffled sobbing. I could see everyone there, but they could not see me and no one reacted to my presence.

Glancing around, I saw a line of mourners filing slowly past a modest casket. The body of a young woman with shoulder-length strawberry-blond hair lay in the casket. Mortuary skills and cosmetics had given her a placid expression; she looked peaceful and beautiful. How sad, I thought—such a young woman robbed of everything earth life had to offer.

My view then focused on an older woman sitting off to one side. She seemed dazed, her eyes staring into space. The pain emanating from her was undeniable. I knew at once that she was the dead woman's mother, hurting, as any parent would when burying one's child. Two beautiful little girls, perhaps four and six years of age, were with her. They were the daughters of the deceased woman—and this woman's grandchildren—and they were sobbing uncontrollably. Their hair had been lovingly done by a caring relative, and they were both dressed in frilly blue dresses with white lace trim.

Somehow I knew that these dresses had been purchased by their dear mother for a happy occasion in the recent past. Now they were being worn for her funeral. The younger child sat on her grandmother's lap, clinging to her and weeping desperately. The six-year-old stood at the side of the grandmother, her face buried in her hands. Her little shoulders shook with her sobs. The children could not stop crying, but their grandmother, in such pain herself that she hardly seemed to realize they were there, was unable to offer comfort.

I understood her thoughts: how was she ever going to take the place of the children's dead mother? She was older, with few financial resources and even fewer physical resources on which to draw. How could she ever love them enough to ease the pain of losing a mother who had left them by choice?

Does Suicide Really Solve Anything?

The dead woman had not died in a tragic accident or of disease. This knowledge came vividly to my mind. She had taken her own life, died by her own actions, voluntarily giving up her chance to accomplish anything more during earth life.

Suddenly I saw the spirit of the young woman kneeling at her mother's feet. She was different from the others in the chapel. Her body was not full and solid like the bodies of her mother and children and the other mourners. She was wispy and transparent, as I myself was at that moment—a spiritual body, not a physical one—and her face was contorted in sorrow and pain. Her mortal body lay a few feet away in the coffin, yet her essence, her spirit, her self was here, sobbing at her mother's knees. I heard her thoughts, her words. She was sorry, oh, so sorry, for what she had done to them. She ached for them and the pain they were experiencing because of her actions.

She reached out, unable to touch them or to be felt by them. Her desperate attempts to make herself heard or understood failed utterly. She tried to take the oldest girl into her arms to comfort her; she wanted to console, to caress her children, but they didn't even know she was there.

I listened as she begged their forgiveness. She was desperate to make them understand, but they could not hear her words. All she could do was watch in torment as they suffered from her actions. I realized she had been a single mother raising these little girls alone. The emotional and physical responsibilities had overwhelmed her; she had come to the point where she felt that her problems and pressures were too great to endure. She felt depressed and allowed her feelings of despondency to grow to the point that she mistakenly felt that release from life was her only solution.

Is Suicide Likely to Free a Person from Emotional Strife?

She had committed suicide, thinking that by so doing she would find peace—and sometime in the future she probably will find forgiveness and peace. But for now, she had found misery instead, as she helplessly watched the pain she had inflicted on the ones she so loved. Instead of being free from emotional strife, she was feeling intensified sorrow, compounded with regret for what she had done to her family. I could sense her agonized frustration. She was unable to communicate with or console her loved ones. She was utterly helpless to aid them in any way.

In suicide, as in all things, only God is the ultimate judge. He will decide the degree to which each person is accountable for his or her actions. For example, people who have a chemical imbalance may not be accountable for their actions. Only God knows. As I watched the scene, my view changed and I envisioned the girls beginning to grow up, raised by their grandmother. Their dead mother continued observing their progress and their pain as they grew up without her. Her torment was great as she saw how they needed her, longed for her, hated her, and dealt with the fact of her abandonment of them (which they perceived as rejection) at every stage of their lives.

She saw her children's sorrow and how she had personally handicapped them. And when they needed her, she was unable to reach them with her love. Physically she was not there for them—never could be there for them. How she longed to hold them! She wished she could undo her death and return to her children. I understood that she would watch not only her children but others in her life who had been wounded by her choice to kill herself.

What Is the Ripple Effect of Suicide?

The analogy of a pebble thrown into a pond came to mind. The ripple that results expands outward and ultimately affects an area immeasurably larger than the size of the pebble itself; the ripple travels on and on. I understood that every action in life, especially suicide, affects so many people that its effect seems endless. The ripples—often more like tidal waves—caused by the deed roll outward, touching many lives.

Having willed myself to die, akin to suicide in my case, I knew that my inner hell would be viewing the loved ones I had left, witnessing the repercussions of my actions. Such thoughts stayed with me throughout my experience. It would be my own personal hell, seeing and not being able to alleviate the sorrow that my actions caused. I was my own judge and was now judging from the spirit world's all-seeing, all-knowing perspective.

The knowledge that I could have done better was agonizing. Seeing my attitudes and actions in the light of truth was misery to my soul. I yearned to warn my family and others of the regret and anguish that I was experiencing. I intensely wanted to return to my mortal life and again have the privilege of living in my physical body, even with its pain and illnesses—even with the same conditions I had sought to escape for so many years.

As quickly as I grasped this, I was shown another scene. Again, I was at a funeral, viewing a person who was deceased. I was standing at the head and slightly behind a beautiful, very expensive casket made of rich rosewood. I knew that this entire funeral had been elaborate and expensive and that the high cost of the funeral was the attempt of grieving parents to soothe their pain.

As I watched, again no one seemed aware of my presence. Before me stood four mortal beings and a spirit personage. I understood at once who each person was and what he or she was feeling. Standing next to me was the spirit personage of a young man. His form, like that of the young mother I had previously seen, was wispy, nearly transparent. He was a good-looking teenager with sandy-colored hair cut short. His natural intelligence was apparent.

An exact duplicate of his form lay in the open casket directly in front of me. I looked from one to the other in amazement. In contrast to his spirit self, his mortal body was solid, still, and lifeless. Its facial features were peaceful, as if he merely slept. His spirit face was contorted with torment and despair. Desperately wanting to make contact, he was reaching out his insubstantial, wispy arms to his father, who was gazing down at the body in the casket. His father's shoulders were stooped with almost unbearable sorrow, his face drawn, his eyes swollen from crying.

Somehow I knew many things about this man. He was close to retirement, with limited financial resources. He had stretched himself beyond his means to make this funeral elaborate, using money from his retirement funds for this final farewell, sparing no expense in an attempt to ease his grief.

The boy's mother stood at the foot of the casket, weeping quietly. Her pain and confusion were profound. The father was speaking softly to two young men; I sensed that they were best friends of the dead boy. Handsome young men, they were intelligent, personable, and well dressed. I realized they were leaders in their classes at school and that they seemed perplexed.

What impressed me as I focused on these two young men was the depth of depression and hopelessness they both had been feeling for some time. The death of the youth did not create their feelings of futility, but simply brought them to the surface—the same feelings the deceased boy had felt when he took his life. I had wasted a large portion of my life feeling the same way.

The father was telling the friends that his

dead son had been a troubled boy with many problems. He looked down at his son's body and rested his hand on the edge of the casket as he said, "He's at peace now." This was what the mourning friends and family wanted to hear. These words eased their sorrow and made this loss easier to bear.

"No, Dad!" the boy's spirit cried out. "Stop! Don't tell them that." I watched as his spirit tried desperately to gain his father's attention, and with horror I realized why he was trying so hard to communicate with his dad.

The bereaved father continued talking about his son's having gone to a better and happier place. He told them his son was free from the pain and depression he felt while alive. I realized that the father's words, which he wanted to believe were true, were giving thoughts of false hope to the two young friends that they could find peace if they, too, committed suicide.

For these boys, the father's words were an invitation to join their friend—a confirmation of what they wanted to be true. They wished to believe that their friend was finally at peace, was finally free from his problems and sadness. They hoped that they, too, could find that peace. The father's words of self-comfort reinforced that message.

But their dead friend was trying with all his might to communicate to them that he was not at peace. He could see the way his friends were feeling—the father could not. Each boy was struggling within, making the decision whether to continue in a life he felt was hopeless or to kill himself and find this beckoning peace. The spirit boy faced his friends in frustration, knowing they couldn't hear him. I heard him wail, his fists clenched, as he tried to communicate with them and convince them not to believe what his father was saying. "My father is wrong, so wrong," he kept saying.

What Is the Lie of "Peace Through Suicide"?

The father continued speaking about how his son had wanted peace and freedom from worldly cares and now he had it. The son's spirit facial features became even more contorted as he shrieked, "No peace! I have no peace!" He was futilely trying to communicate with his father, trying to warn his friends not to make the same mistake. If they did, he knew his misery would be even worse.

Feelings of misery seemed to emanate from him. He had taken his own life, falsely believing that in death he would find happiness, peace, and contentment. He thought he could escape from all earthly anxiety. Instead he found feelings of intense sorrow and anguish that were greater than any he had experienced when he was alive.

He began sobbing, and I observed that he found absolutely no comfort in the beautiful funeral. Instead he felt great misery at the "reassuring" words his father spoke. He understood clearly that it wasn't only these two close friends that would be affected by his actions and his father's words.

Is Suicide Ever the Answer?

If one or both of these boys chose to die, family, other friends, peers, and schoolmates would be affected. Even strangers who would hear about such deaths or read the obituaries might be swayed into thinking suicide could be a solution. I saw how feelings of hopelessness could compound, affecting many people, sweeping relentlessly onward like waves driven by storms far across the ocean.

I felt great sorrow for the dead boy who had given up his chance at earth life, for the friends who were seriously contemplating taking their own lives, and for the parents who had invested so much time and love in their son. A feeling of anguish swept over me, and I wanted to run away as I recognized how my own life fit a pattern similar to what I had been shown. I felt overwhelmed with feelings of guilt, and I knew that suicide was not the answer!

Is Suicide a Sin?

Thinking suicidal thoughts, as I had so many times, often leads to the act of committing suicide. Suicide is like a disease that kills some and often cripples everyone else involved. Suicide and the hopeless feelings of depression connected to it snowball from sad individual to sad individual. Suicide begins cycles of negative thoughts and feelings that create misery throughout generations, robbing posterity and all concerned of great might-have-beens of joy, accomplishment, and peace of mind.

Did Your Life Pass Before Your Eyes?

Once I grasped these eternal truths, suddenly and with lightning speed my whole life began unfolding before me. I felt again the emotions I had experienced during the actual times I first lived them, and yet I was aware of the overall circumstances, aware that I was now in a different time and spiritual domain than on earth when they first took place.

Instead of the limited perspective I'd had on earth, this experience encompassed the feelings and viewpoints of all those involved, including those of the Creator. With this perspective came a stark, resounding realization: life had not been the way it was portrayed in movies, books, songs, or newspapers. Life had not been as I had perceived it at all!

In the spiritual sphere, I had a new, sharp awareness of reality. My life review continued, bringing with it an awareness of those with whom I had associated throughout my life. I was aware of the way they felt about my actions and our interactions. The review was difficult but informative. I was amused to realize that many situations I had thought were serious at the time were really not serious at all. I felt sincere sadness when I revisited the points in my life where I could have done much better.

Although moving with incredible speed, as though someone had put my life on super fast-forward, I quickly discovered that I could linger on any scene that caught my interest, reexperiencing it moment by moment if I desired. My life review was extremely enlightening and continued to be supplemented by a series of scenes that were allegories and parables—a unique teaching experience tailored to my particular needs.

In life, I had been argumentative, especially with my mother. The review revealed clearly how foolish and hurtful all those conflicts had been. Experiencing others' feelings as well as my own during turbulent episodes was a painful, humbling revelation.

Does Repentance Erase Wrongdoing?

At that thought, I realized that wrong deeds for which I had felt remorse and repented of were not in my life review. Those things were gone!

Vividly, however, I realized I could have repented for the wrong deeds I was still seeing, such as seeking revenge, being easily provoked, or doing things that worked against my own life's progression. If only I had been more forgiving, more accepting during my lifetime, how much pain could have been spared, not only then but now, in this moment of realization!

What Does God Expect from Us?

Suddenly everything I had learned and seen was surrounding me in this sphere of endlessness. I was aware again of the presence of the Being of Light and His love that continued to radiate and powerfully encircle me. I knew with all my heart that He loved me in spite of the mistakes I had made in my life. His love was complete, all-knowing, and unconditional.

A great question then emanated from Him to me so strongly that it completely penetrated my being: "In life, what did you do with what you had?" The question engulfed me, demanding an answer.

I began answering defensively, giving reasons and excuses, as I had in life when I felt I was being called to task for failure to reach a goal. It was easy to find someone or something to blame for my failures. I could justify myself with reasons other than my own shortcomings for my actions, feelings, or failure to accomplish certain tasks.

I believed my excuses were good reasons to explain why I hadn't accomplished more: my difficult childhood, others getting in my way, my poor health, a broken home, my continual strife with my mother, lack of opportunities, and my growing family of children who held me back.

More excuses welled up within me. If only I had been blessed with strong, supportive parents and raised in an atmosphere of love and acceptance. If only I'd had a happy, successful marriage. If only I'd had more money.

I was stopped short in my thinking as I felt all my excuses melting in this light of truth. I felt the thoughts and words coming from this Being of Love and Light. "The question has nothing to do with what you did not have in life or with your burdens or faults or problems. It has only to do with this: In life what did you do with what you did have?"

Oh, the humility and the guilt I felt at that moment. All of my life's actions were seen and known. I couldn't hide them or cover them. My carefully erected walls of excuses that had shielded me from accepting responsibility melted around me. All that was left was just me and the Being of Love and Light who knew everything about me.

I could not rely on or blame anyone else. This question was directed solely at me. I was being measured against no one else—I stood alone, on my own. What did I do with my life, with what

I had, my opportunities, my time on earth? What had I done with what I did have?

Suddenly I realized that difficulties during earth life were really opportunities. I recognized how problems could be blessings when viewed from the Other Side.

How Are Our Lives Judged?

On earth the goal is to win; it is certainly the overriding desire of sports teams and corporations. Winning is the measure of success during earth life; winning means fame and money. Losers are remembered only if the circumstances are humorous, sad, or if the loss is embarrassingly big. We all energetically avoid the label of "loser" from childhood on.

Competition is fierce in most aspects of mortal life—from entrance requirements to college to parking spaces at the shopping mall. I was amazed to realize that in the afterlife sphere there is no win or lose, no competition with anyone else. The only thing that mattered was what I did with what I had. What I did not have was irrelevant.

If only I had known to teach my family to do the best they could without the emphasis on winning or losing—to pay attention to how they lived. Life is like a game in a way, but the score that matters is determined not by wins and losses according to the world's standard but by doing the best we can with what we have.

I now understood that there was no real defeat on earth. Only my own choices of attitudes and actions mattered. The important thing was to keep going, to look for solutions, to strive and endure well until the end of life, to desire and to keep trying to live in harmony with eternal truths. I realized the need for everyone to help the world be a better place for those living, as well as for future generations.

Are There "If Onlys" on the Other Side?

In many ways what I had *not* done with my life seemed more significant than what I *had* done to this point. I knew that every day I had lived on earth I had exchanged a day of potential for whatever I had chosen to do that day. Many days I had done nothing, and now I saw what I had thrown away.

There is eternal joy to be reaped from seeking to do kind deeds and from not being easily offended, on earth and for eternity. I realized that we don't have to be perfect during earth life; we just need to be sincerely caring and make an effort to become more loving, charitable, and forgiving—and less judgmental. The desires and intent of the heart are so significant. You cannot lose this game so long as you continue to play.

As I understood the purpose of earth life from an eternal perspective, I became aware that miracles happened abundantly and more easily for those who believed in them. Also, I knew that my station or level of life was not as important as the direction I was going and whether or not I was moving toward eternal goals, appreciating opportunities, and striving to improve.

On the Other Side, I learned that trying counts and all sincere efforts are recognized with accompanying just rewards. My life review showed me with complete clarity that every choice I had made in attitude, thought, or action had an inescapable consequence, wanted or unwanted. I alone was responsible for what I had done with my life.

Why Is Life so Unfair?

Before my experience on the Other Side, I had not understood reasons for burdens and adversities. It seemed unfair that so many trials and problems brought so much grief during earth life. I wondered why some people had such dreadful lives of hardship, and others seemed to have relatively few problems. I learned that the answers could not be obtained by viewing a short period of time in one's life on earth. But from the perspective of the Other Side, which included everyone's feelings and viewpoint—even the Creator's—everything fits together.

Rich rewards and priceless joy await humble people on earth who valiantly suffer through their trials and tribulations.

Knowledge came to my mind about people who were born with less than I had. I understood that though we are not born into equal situations we all have many more opportunities than we realize. I then knew that many of those who seem to have little according to the world's standards have the opportunity of reaping great rewards on the Other Side.

I learned that adversities are opportunities for personal growth and development and come with built-in benefits that can be enjoyed endlessly. I discovered that justice during earth life is usually found only in the dictionary. Almost everyone on earth is seeking justice, but justice means different things to different people. What is just to one person is unjust to another. On the Other Side, however, there is complete justice. I recognized how important mercy is and how much more it can be received on earth when it is freely given.

Is God to Blame for Our Circumstances?

I understood that God permits us to make our own choices concerning our attitudes, actions, and especially reactions. God does not force us to do what is right during earth life, and we do not have the right to force someone else to do "right" or to make "right decisions"; earth life is a time to learn from choices.

I realized, however, that even though God is saddened when we make choices that bring heartache or grief to ourselves or others, He still safeguards our free will to make these decisions. I remembered times during my earth life when I had blamed God for my circumstances and my unhappiness. With this new understanding and perspective, I realized that most of my experiences on earth were the consequences of my choices or my family's choices. Regardless of the difficulties, I could triumph over them with lasting results on the Other Side.

What Happens if We Don't Repent?

My understanding was opened further as I became aware of some of the ways repentance works, and of the just and terrible consequences that may await on the Other Side for those who do not strive to use their earth time wisely and repent of their wrongdoing. When someone intentionally wrongs another, what awaits them is a confrontation of their improper actions and a full realization of their guilt and their lost rewards. I discovered, however, that blessings and joy can be received by taking the opportunity to repent and do differently while we are still alive on earth and have choices.

Earth life, I found, is designed as a university, a school where we learn from our choices and our mortal experiences. I recognized that my most painful experiences taught me the most. It was enlightening to understand the bigger eternal picture—to know that I was not a victim of circumstances. I learned that I could control my attitude and ultimately, my heavenly rewards.

How Can We Keep Life's Problems in Perspective?

Suddenly an analogy came to my mind about problems and the difficulty of seeing them from a proper perspective. I wanted to tell my loved ones about a coping technique I'd learned—putting an object the size of a quarter to one eye while closing the other and then likening that object to a problem. It would be so close that they could see only the object—the problem. Viewed in this manner, problems can become overwhelming and can conceal obvious solutions.

Next, I envisioned light beginning to appear around the edges of the object as the hand holding it moved slowly away from the eye. Soon the object was far enough away that the things around it could be seen in perspective according to how it fit in and influenced the rest of life. Solutions could now be seen that had been there all the time but had been concealed, eclipsed by the problem when it was out of perspective.

I immediately recognized this as a symbolic visual parable of my own life. Problems would have seemed less devastating to me if I had been able to stand back and view each one in its eternal perspective. Answers would have presented themselves. Solutions would have become more obvious.

I realized I had grown wiser as a result of my problems and earthly trials. But I saw that I could have gotten through situations, problems, and crises easier, and been much further ahead in life, if I had envisioned the end result of my actions instead of staying caught up in the problem.

Knowing What You Know, Would You Trade Problems with Anyone Else?

Then I thought of times I had looked at people who seemed to be free of problems. Sometimes I had even wished I could trade places with some of them and have the life of peace and ease that I mistakenly thought they had.

In the spirit sphere, a story I'd heard on earth about comparing other people's problems to my own vividly came to my mind. My consciousness was filled with scenes of this visual parable. I saw myself sitting in a roomful of people who were successful and free of problems when measured by worldly standards.

We were passing around a large, dark-colored, expandable bag, and all the people were stuffing their problems into it. As they filled the bag, I could see their trials and challenges, which had previously been hidden from my view. I realized that if I'd really known these people, I would have known that they, too, had problems that seemed as difficult to them as my own did to me. Many of them had even more problems than I did.

As soon as they had all placed their problems in the bag, it was tossed into the center of the room. The bag popped open, and all the problems began spilling out. Instantly, everyone scrambled to reclaim their own. I dashed in among them, suddenly desperate to find my own set of familiar problems and trials. I did not want anyone else's—only my own.

I now realized that my problems were my own personal educational building blocks, tailored just for me. Learning from my problems—the cause and effect of my choices, and my parents', and their parents' before them could help me overcome undesired social, cultural, or family traditions.

Suddenly I knew I would not want to trade places with anyone else. I needed to grow and develop in my own way, which was different from any other person's way. Someone else's life experiences would not help me to become the individual that I needed to be. I needed my own individualized training.

I now knew that facing challenges builds the

"muscles and strengths" of spirit and mind. Only through such exercises could I have developed as I needed to do. To build physical muscles, we lift weights. To develop the "muscles" of mind and spirit, we have the chance to solve problems, grow wise through them, and gain skills, knowledge, and talents that remain with us forever.

I understood now that the more people learn and apply on earth, the more advantage they gain on the Other Side. I realized that when I died, I left behind all material wealth and worldly goods. They didn't really matter anymore—people mattered. I became vividly aware of how important people are, especially one's own family.

With my expanded knowledge, I also knew the importance of learning and developing skills of patience and communication with family and others in earth life; there are endless benefits in the spiritual sphere. I learned that charity, patience, and forgiveness toward others are some of the most important character traits to be acquired—learned—from the school of life.

My perspective had changed completely. These scenes brought me priceless learning experiences, but my learning had just begun.

Can We Really "Coast Through Life"?

More thoughts came to my mind about lessons I'd learned from troublesome situations. I thought of times when I'd wanted to stay on a plateau. I heard myself saying, "No more growth, God, please. Let me just stay where I am. Please let me rest through a nice coasting period." Instantly, I realized that there's no such thing as coasting—I was either going forward in life, acquiring good habits, or I was going backward, acquiring bad habits, such as being impatient or developing an "I don't care" attitude.

What Is the Point of "Learning Experiences"?

Returning to scenes from my life review, I was struck by the realization that daily or routine tasks presented opportunities for strengthening personal characteristics of patience and understanding for others. Previously, when people did things I thought were rude—such as crowding in a ticket line or cutting in front of me in traffic—my desire for justice surfaced and I felt compelled to express my views to them verbally, whether they could hear me or not.

I watched many of my actions and reactions. Most of the time when I got behind the wheel to drive, I was in a hurry and thought of driving merely as getting from point A to point B. Anything that happened along the way to delay me sparked my anger.

When I observed these scenes from this new perspective, knowing my feelings and also many of the other people's feelings and attitudes, it suddenly seemed foolish and childish to react impulsively and point out others' faults on the highway or anyplace else. I no longer wanted to judge others' motives. I knew the drivers did not realize the full consequences of their actions, as I had not previously, and that impulsive actions could lead to deadly accidents with ripple effects that could cause great anguish.

Driving a vehicle, I saw, was one of many routine tasks that present opportunities to develop good character traits. It was also a definite "mini-test" of character—of how we think, act, and react toward others when it seems no one is watching or when we think our actions are not really important. Driving in congested traffic can be a great opportunity to build patience.

All situations and challenges, I saw, can be

learning experiences. I could have reaped benefits if, when faced with a challenge, I had asked myself, "What can I learn from this situation?" Also, I discovered that it had been a waste of time trying to wish away my challenges, problems, and trials; they were my "spiritual muscle builders."

Coping techniques I could have used in my life became easier for me to understand. I saw that I could have taken a problem or a difficult situation and examined its significance a hundred years from now by asking myself who would have been affected by it, and how. Given that much time, did it still seem major or was it now minor? Taking that problem and sending it one hundred years into the future, how big or how small did it become? Could I even see it? Did it really matter in the outcome of my life? Many of my problems would have shrunk immediately if I had envisioned them in those terms.

Is It Okay Just to Wait Out the Bad Times?

Life comes in phases, I realized, and each phase seems to stretch out in earth years as if it will last forever—but it never does. Earth time is not forever. Situations come and go, trials pass. If you can keep your spirits high and refuse to give in to despair, then this, too, shall pass.

I thought again of the young woman and the teenage boy who had committed suicide. If they had waited, things might have improved for them. It was tragic that by not realizing this, they had both taken actions that had ended their earthly growth forever and utterly stifled their spiritual life.

Is Life Ever Truly Unbearable?

My life review continued, and I saw that I had received great blessings, more than I knew. I was surprised as I became aware of times when my life and my children's lives had been spared, and I realized that everyone on earth has many more blessings and miracles than they recognize at the time.

Repeatedly, I realized that things in my life could have been much worse than they had been. When I was caught up in what went wrong, I overlooked the things that went right and the many blessings I had received.

One fact became clear: I found what I looked

for. I learned it is better to look for and find things that have gone right—the many blessings received. I saw that by acknowledging and expressing gratitude for blessings received, even more would be given. I realized that life itself and each day of it had been a gift—if only I had noticed.

What Is the Real Test of Life?

It seemed as if a light had suddenly gone on. I understood that if problems could bring blessings and opportunities, then the real test in my life was the intent of my heart and whether or not I had the right attitude. Even in situations that had gone badly for me, I could have passed the test if I'd had good intentions and the right attitude.

It became obvious that there were many times in my life when I had succeeded—such as times I had held my tongue and not argued when someone was verbally venting frustrations as if I had been the cause of the problem. Joyfully, I was aware of some other times that I had kept good thoughts and intentions when it was extremely difficult to do so.

I realized that living in the world and accepting the tests throughout life build character for eternity. Life is somewhat like a game—but the score is actually kept more on the Other Side than on the earth and is based on what we do with what we have. There is no competition with anyone else. When my life review showed that I had passed some difficult test in life, I was filled with joy.

As knowledge filled my mind, I knew that each of my adversities carried with it a seed of opportunity for growth and improvement. But I needed faith to recognize and continue with patience until the growth was realized. That was the challenge—to persist and look for the good.

On the Other Side, the definite revelation came to me that I had had more opportunities than I realized while I was alive and situations could have improved. Then I knew that where I had been in earth life was not as important as the direction in which I had been going.

Also, I learned that problems can refine the spirit—as I said before, they are spiritual muscle builders. I realized that all kinds of coping techniques are available on earth if only we open our minds and hearts to them.

But now I believed it was too late for me to utilize the knowledge that I had gained. Being dead was so final! I could no longer have any impact on earth life.

Why Do People Hurt Each Other So Much in Life?

On earth, my tremendous determination to push for fairness and justice in the world led me to have an argumentative attitude.

On the Other Side, knowledge about communication and relationships poured into my consciousness. Scenes from eternity that I was shown seemed personalized for my instruction. Perhaps that is why I was shown many scenes about arguing, the futility of it, and the damage it causes to relationships.

At one point in my view from the Other Side, I saw couples involved in heated disputes, shouting at each other. I watched, sharing their thoughts, feelings, and emotions as they argued. It was almost as though I could step inside each person's mind and heart and know what he or she was experiencing.

I was amazed as I observed what was happening: the words they spoke were completely different from the feelings they had. It was clear that they did not know how to communicate what they felt toward each other or how to explain their feelings without verbally attacking each other. Obviously they did not understand each other's viewpoints.

Also, what they wanted from their partner was not manifest in what they were saying. In fact, as they argued they strayed far from the original conflict. Their accusations became more outrageous, their demands more and more inappropriate, and they eventually resorted to name-calling. All the while, each partner was feeling hurt and shocked that his or her loved one's words and responses were as unkind as his or her own.

One woman spewed verbal threats at her mate, such as "If you leave me, I'll take the children so far away you'll never see them again," and, "If you leave, I'll find someone so much better than you." But what she was actually thinking was that she loved her husband and wanted to put her arms around him and calm things for them both; she desperately wanted him to put his arms around her and tell her that he loved her. Not knowing her true feelings, he reacted to her words and felt totally rejected.

She didn't see that when she hurled angry words at him, she was sowing more anger. As certain as planted seeds yield their own kind, he responded to her hateful words with hateful words of his own—and she was hurt even more. His response was so different from what she wanted that she threw back even more bitter words and threats. The wrangling continued and pointlessly escalated. Their feelings were easy to perceive. They were both bewildered and wondered why the other person hurled back hurtful, vindictive words that surprised and further angered them.

As I shared their feelings, I knew that these arguments and angry emotions grew because of the frustration of not knowing what to say, what to do, or how to respond to the other's behavior. They simply did not know how to express themselves so the other person could understand their viewpoint.

I knew that neither the woman nor her mate meant the things they were saying; each reacted to what the other was saying without thinking of the consequences. They could not separate themselves from the contention long enough to act the way they wanted to. Instead, they trapped themselves in their arguments.

They each felt enormous heartache and emotional pain. I wanted to shout to them, to tell them to stop and listen to what they were saying. If one of them would take time to think about the situation and understand what the other was really feeling, they could have changed everything. If either one of them had stopped criticizing the other and had stopped attacking the other at the most vulnerable points, the argument could have stopped, and irreparable damage to each other's feelings and their relationship could have been avoided.

I learned that most arguments are futile. They come from limited understanding of others and from limited communication skills. If a situation could be viewed from all dimensions, including the perspectives of others, and if people could control their words, arguments would dwindle or even cease. Sincere empathy and unconditional love would replace the inclination to argue or to hurt another person.

Is Listening Enough to Stop Someone from Hurting?

The importance and wisdom of listening with an understanding heart and communicating without criticizing and putting others down was impressed upon my mind as I understood the far-reaching consequences and effects of words.

I understood that things would have been different if any of the people I had seen fighting had simply been strong enough to look compassionately at the other person, quietly listen, and accept their partner's opinions without contradiction. Each had an opinion, at a certain level of growth. Each wanted understanding of his or her opinion, to be heard nonjudgmentally, to feel loved and accepted. They did not want instructions about what to do or unasked-for solutions.

Each partner needed to see things from the other's point of view without criticizing and or putting down the other. I thought of times when I had been in similar situations. The wealth of people skills that had been important and available to me on earth was now vividly apparent in the spiritual realm, where I was shown the truth.

I became aware of some of the challenges of women involved in arguments because their mates wanted only their own opinions or decisions to be accepted as the final word, with no discussion or allowance for expression of a differing viewpoint, opinion, or expansion on their ideas. This need caused some women to feel frustrated and to develop pent-up feelings of anger. Other women unleashed harsh words that fueled heated arguments.

Yet I knew relationships on earth could be revitalized if people would only keep in mind the answer to the question: "How important will this argument be in one hundred years? Even in one hundred days?"

Another couple I saw arguing was, again, one spouse trying to change the other's opinion. I could see that their argument was a waste of time. The more the man bickered and badgered and belittled his wife, the stronger she came back at him with her opinions and accusations. I could feel what she was feeling and I understood why she believed the way she did.

The wife was at a different level of growth than her husband was. She thought she was absolutely justified in her beliefs. He, on the other hand, was coming from his own stage of growth and beliefs. He was feeling greatly frustrated, and he could not comprehend why his wife couldn't see his point of view. Childishly, neither person would step back and allow the other to have a different opinion. They didn't even try to see the situation from the other person's viewpoint, and they would not let go of their own opinions.

Why Is "Proving Who's Right" a Futile Exercise?

I learned an important concept: Let it go. I realized how much energy is wasted in trying to prove oneself right. Arguing over ideas and opinions can ruin relationships. As each person uses words that hurt, it is as if he or she is lighting the fires of anger in the other. Harsh words only add to the other person's anger and he or she becomes more inflamed—it is like trying to put out a fire by throwing gasoline on it. Leaving opinions unchallenged can be much wiser.

Watching these couples argue while feeling their real emotions myself gave me new understandings, patience, and acceptance of the opinions of others. It helped me realize how much time I had wasted in contention and argument. I became aware that being unwilling to see another's viewpoint or not taking time to communicate so that another understands properly always damages relationships.

Can Words Really Make a Difference When Things Are Bad?

More knowledge came into my mind, and I became aware of many benefits of loving unconditionally—especially the importance of expressing loving words. I knew that people need to feel loved and to be told that they are loved. Sincere loving words can be a healing balm to the soul of someone who is hurting.

Thoughts came to my mind of some of the many times in my life when I had yearned to feel loved. I knew that I was not alone. Usually women, even more than men, long to hear those precious words, "I love you."

I wondered why it was so difficult for most men to understand women's feelings, why it was usually difficult for them to express loving words. With that thought, it was as though I could see through a man's eyes and feel with a man's heart. I suddenly knew how different men's perspectives are from women's and how extremely difficult it can be for them to understand women. With this new awareness, I realized how difficult it is for most men to express their feelings. Generally it is easier and more natural for women to talk about what bothers them.

Men usually don't know what a woman means when she says she doesn't feel loved, or when she wants to discuss all the things that upset her. Men usually believe they are showing love by working hard for their families, and they often think that loving words are unnecessary. Usually the man does not know how to respond and may withdraw—the opposite response to what the woman wants.

I realized that some of this lack came from the example of parents who did not express their feelings—patterns handed down from generation to generation. Also, the sexes were created with definite differences in temperament and emotions for many good reasons. I knew, however, that situations and people can change as they react and adapt to each other's differences.

Does Anyone Ever Really Win an Argument?

From these scenes I viewed on the Other Side, I became aware that quarreling over differences does not lead to solutions and arguments are never actually "won." If a "victory" hurts another, it is no real victory. The couples I saw arguing did not have clear goals; arguing had become a habit and was destructive to the self-esteem of those involved—especially to the tender feelings of children.

The people in these arguments did not realize that they displayed their own faults when they raised their voices for emphasis, shouted, and used profanity to make an impression. It was observable that they were without adequate words in their vocabulary and that they were trying to sound smarter, more "right," speaking in this manner. Being unwilling or unable to communicate effectively, they shouted put-downs instead.

At times they laughed at others, or became angry, or labeled them "stupid" for not agreeing with their opinions or for not following their instructions. They did not see that the failing was their own—they were not communicating adequately.

As I watched these couples locked in useless arguing, I knew the feelings of each partner and became aware that people skills—especially communication skills—are a vital part of the mortal experience. Whether or not we choose to learn them will have far-reaching effects.

Is Justice Ever Truly Handed Out?

In my life review, I saw times where I had been offended or hurt by someone and also times when I had been the one causing an offense. I watched the way I acted or reacted. I experienced the same thoughts and felt the feelings I had at those moments, and I knew the thoughts and experienced the feelings of other individuals involved. This gave me a profound new awakening and awareness of my senses, and my consciousness was filled with understanding of our motivations. At the time, I had misjudged others because I did not know their viewpoints. I regretted making a big issue of seeking justice. I had wanted those who seemed to hurt others deliberately to pay for their behavior.

I was critical and would get upset when people who seemed cruel or unfair to others prospered from their ruthlessness. I thought that they did not have many trials or tribulations, but led happy lives. In contrast, I wondered why many humble, kind people seemed to trudge through life having to bear numerous hardships.

What Happens if Someone Is Violent and Hurts Someone Else?

When my awareness was expanded to view situations in their proper eternal perspective, I knew that after someone had lived his or her life and gone to the Other Side, he or she would face all earthly actions, and no one would get ahead unfairly. Good deeds, small and large, would be rewarded. Things would be fair on the other side.

I realized that earth time had been my time for gathering kind thoughts, deeds, and actions for enjoyment on the Other Side. I wish I could adequately describe my feelings, the sorrow I experienced when I realized I had criticized or misjudged another of God's children in some way during my journey through life. In instances where I'd hurt another's feelings, I felt deep remorse.

Also, I knew that if someone hurts another and seems to get away with it, apparently cheating justice while alive on earth, there is no need to wish revenge on them. If a person does not seem to have a conscience on earth, it does not mean that he or she does not have one; on the contrary such people do, and it will pain them with great agony later. They are really hurting themselves.

Instead of being relieved or grateful that others would someday have to pay for their behavior, however, I felt sorrow for them as I realized that they were losing their Other Side rewards and bringing punishment on themselves. With my new and increased understanding of eternal rewards and eternal punishments, I no longer wanted revenge or retaliation against anyone for anything. I knew that it was a great universal truth that what we give out comes back to us. As we judge others, we will be judged. As we sow, so shall we reap.

Is Kindness Really Its Own Best Reward?

Then the thought came forcefully to my mind that if what I give out is truly what I get back, I didn't want justice. I wanted mercy! I knew now that if I had wanted to receive mercy, I would have had to give mercy while I was alive. I wanted to return to earth life and be merciful to others. Also, I knew that if I had intentionally offended one of God's children, it was an offense to God.

I knew for myself what I had done or not done on earth, and glorious feelings of joy accompanied the good I had done, especially for those who seemed to deserve it least.

More knowledge came to my mind with a sharp awareness of truth about the importance of being kind and merciful not only to people but to all of God's creatures: animals, birds, reptiles, and so on. God's love extends to His creatures in all their wondrous variety, and so should ours. I knew that they were placed on earth for wise purposes and that they were not to be intentionally mistreated.

All of the knowledge I had been shown added to my understanding of the importance of the time on earth and the joy I could have reaped if I had spent more of my time giving mercy rather than seeking justice.

Abruptly, I was again aware of the question from the Being of Light. As He repeated it to me, it pierced my consciousness. He asked, "What did you do with what you had in life?" This question had nothing to do with blessings that other people received in their lives, or what others had done with their circumstances in life. Rather, I absolutely knew again that I was not competing against anyone else for good works; there was no one else to blame for my omissions. He was asking me only what I had done with what I did have. My sins of omission became very obvious to me—there were things I did not do that I should have done with what I was given, such as being more charitable, patient, and helpful to others.

My chance at mortal life's opportunities to grow mentally and spiritually was over. I wanted to run, to hide—anything to avoid facing the reality that I'd not done what I could have during my earth life. But I knew that what I was experiencing resulted from my own thoughts and actions on earth.

Then I thought of some of the little good deeds I had done for others that only they and I knew about, such as when I took time to cheer and visit someone who needed encouragement, especially when it was not convenient for me. These were things that I thought to be insignificant at the time.

In the spiritual realm, however, I was benefiting from those small acts of kindness in a much larger way. The joy I received from my little kind deeds was magnified, and I realized that God is pleased when one of His children helps another one. Precious feelings of joy flooded me, and I knew that all compassionate acts of charity and kindness, even small ones, reap joy and great rewards. I also understood the importance of true, unconditional love for others. Every word or action motivated by love, not because someone did something for me first, brought peace to my soul.

I knew God had set the example for us by loving every one of us unconditionally. As I thought of this, my being was infused again with total love from the Personage of Love and Light. I felt love radiate from Him all through and around me. His love was so magnificent that it vastly expanded my feelings of love and empathy for others. I marveled that I could feel that deeply, that anyone could feel that much love.

As more knowledge expanded my consciousness, it became clear that a higher way of living could be accomplished on earth. It required that people make constant choices to avoid condemning, gossiping, criticizing, and judging others.

Even though it would be a continual day-to-day challenge for most everyone, I knew there would be more lasting happiness while living on earth for those who strive to avoid judging others. Family patterns and personal traits of love and forgiveness could be handed down to posterity by example, and all could reap eternal rewards.

I became aware that appreciating others and their differences promotes creativity and diversity and enjoyment. It became clear that there are differences in people's preferences and their actions according to their age, experience, and family influence. I knew it would be sad if we all had the same likes and dislikes; things would look dull if everyone wanted the same color and kind of cars, houses, or clothes. Suddenly I knew that diversity makes the world an interesting and colorful place.

Then I knew that accepting people at their own level of growth and patiently letting them learn from their choices can bring peace and joy beyond description. Acceptance would bring a form of freedom—freedom from pettiness, from prejudice, from judging and being judged. The freedom I felt was wonderful as I understood that each person has different interests and goals and was to be permitted to learn from the results of his or her choices.

More knowledge came to my mind, that there are immeasurable benefits of not judging people's actions, looks, or differences. I understood that when people felt accepted and were permitted to choose freely, they could more easily grow to their personal potential.

At this point, I was understanding things from the perspective of eternal growth, viewing all phases of a situation, all sides, along with the feelings of those involved. I could see the results, the repercussions of my wrongful decisions or indecisions.

My thoughts turned to the Scriptures, and I was impressed with their truthfulness, beauty, and the rewards to be gained by learning and striving to live God's teachings. I was amazed to realize how literally true and wise the Scriptures are. I knew that just reading their words could never do them justice, but by pondering them, I could recognize more of their meaning.

Can We Fool God?

My every action or reaction, I found, went out in time like unending circles that somehow came back to me. There was no way to edit what had occurred or to make it go away. Anything I did or did not do for anyone else had an effect that came back to me. I could no more fool God into thinking I had done my best with my time on earth than I could fool myself.

Now I wanted to return to my body on earth to apply what I had learned. I wanted desperately to be able to speak. I felt that if I were given the chance to tell others, I would shout from the rooftops what I had learned: the importance of being forgiving and the countless blessings that can be reaped by being kind, merciful, and unconditionally loving.

Still, I believed that my plea was in vain. I had made my choice. The saddest experience I ever had was to recognize all the things I could no longer do and to know that I could not make any corrections to my choices. I was racked with torment as I realized that I could no longer even attempt to repent and do better in life.

●

Must We Forgive to Be Forgiven?

I knew that there were many benefits of being forgiving and that if I wanted to be forgiven for actions that I regretted, I would need to be forgiving of others during my earth life. I wanted to be able to forgive anyone and everyone who had offended me. I discovered that it was literally true that we earn what we receive on the Other Side by the choices we make while on the earth. As I experienced my life review and understood things in their proper perspective, I saw that each time I had wished justice on another I was determining the way I would judge myself.

On earth, I had taken classes that taught a false process for getting over offenses: First, tell those involved how much they had hurt me. Second, talk it out. Third, receive an apology from the offender(s), and fourth, let it go. But I was mistakenly told that I was to receive an apology from the offender before I moved on.

When my knowledge was expanded, to my

surprise I discovered I was not to tell someone how I felt about them and then forgive them. I was to forgive others unconditionally and treat them as I would want to be treated, not just for their sake, but for mine, because of how I would feel about myself and my actions. Forgiving, forgetting, and letting go of grudges brings benefits for all concerned, whether or not offenders apologize and ask for forgiveness.

Knowing that the sooner I rid myself of feeling offended, the better off I would be, I saw that I could have gained peace of mind in the mortal world and had more peace in the spiritual realm if I'd done this. I knew that anger at anyone hurt me mentally, physically, and especially spiritually.

Even though there was a different sense of "time" on the Other Side, I realized I had learned a lot and had seen many scenes since my transition from earth life to the spirit world. At that time, I thought that I might be caught forever in this awful state where I was filled with feelings of remorse.

Suddenly I felt myself moving through a space of dense blackness and through the midst of miserable souls who had died while still holding on to angry, bitter grudges toward others. They carried their dark, angry feelings with them in the spirit realm, and they could not let go of them. Wanting to escape the angry feelings, I found myself floating away from the darkness and through space. Coming down through a beam of light, I found myself looking into a room in a hospital. I saw an older man lying in a hospital bed blankly staring toward the end of his bed and upward toward the ceiling.

I wondered if he could see me looking down on him, but then I knew he could not. Drifting into and out of consciousness, he was too weak to move or communicate with the man and woman standing at the side of his bed. By mental communication, I knew that the woman about his same age was his wife, and the younger man was his son.

Also I realized that the father had been very angry with his son and had not spoken to him for years, except with extremely harsh words. The mother and son felt that his bad feelings had added to the deterioration of the father's health. The son had avoided further contact, and each believed the other should apologize. Now, with the father's impending death, there was great sadness displayed on the faces and in the words of the mother and son. Tears rolled down the son's cheeks, and his voice broke as he said, "Dad, I'm so sorry for hurting you. Please forgive me. I love you. Please forgive me, Dad." He repeated the words many times, as he cried and asked for forgiveness.

I understood the son's sorrow. He knew it was too late; his father was dying and could not respond. But the young man continued trying to make himself heard and to apologize. It was easy to observe that the young man felt tremendous guilt knowing he had waited too long to speak the precious words his father wanted to hear but that he could not previously bring himself to say: "I am sorry. I love you."

The son turned toward his mother and tearfully said, "Mom, I am so sorry for not apologizing to Dad before. I know I have hurt us all. I am sorry I wasn't there when Dad needed me." He turned back to his father and continued crying and apologizing but still with no response from the father.

The mother lowered her head as she too, cried softly. I understood her pained emotions; she felt torn between her son and her husband, and she had lost the enjoyment of them both over this family feud. Her sadness was intensified now, for the two of them and for herself.

Watching them, I wondered how long this young man would feel these terrible feelings of remorse. I did not receive an answer, but I recognized many of my own foolish feelings, when I had been involved in futile arguments and waited for another person to apologize. I now saw the value of putting a relationship ahead of receiving words of apology.

Many people, I now knew, feel offended and wait for others to take the first step in the forgiving process—to call and say they are sorry. They wait to hear those priceless words, "I love you." But when they are close to death they have painful feelings of wanting to be able to communicate their love. I knew that when they were finally facing death, they no longer wanted to express anger; rather, they wanted to ask for forgiveness, express love, and feel the other's love in return.

No one on earth knows for sure when their time may unexpectedly run out, when it will be too late to communicate their love. I thought of my own circumstances, and I knew that time is too limited to waste holding grudges, being angry, and withholding love.

What Are the Blessings of Forgiveness?

We take our feelings with us when we die. Those who are patient with others, who are able to forgive when feeling offended and let go of anger on earth, experience great feelings of glorious freedom and inner peace on the Other Side. They reap joy beyond comprehension.

When my understanding was opened, I sincerely sorrowed for those who hold grudges, intentionally hurt another's feelings, or try to take advantage of others. They would not do or say hurtful things if they realized the seemingly unending ripples of repercussions from regrettable actions. Decisions to hurt others result in lost opportunities for reaping joy and eternal peace of mind.

What Is the Connection Between Care of the Body and Heavenly Rewards?

Throughout my life I had struggled to feel confident. I had not been happy with my weight or my appearance. Most of my life I felt I was too heavy or too old or too ill. When I looked in the mirror, my attention focused on my physical imperfections.

On the Other Side, I gained an entirely different impression of my body. When I watched my life review, it became clear what a valuable gift my body was and how necessary it was to accomplish what I desired to do during earth life. I didn't need to be unhappy because I did not look a certain way or was not the same size as someone else. The important thing was that I had a body. It had been dependent on how I treated it; if I had kept it healthy it could have served me well rather than hindered my progress during my life's journey.

In the spiritual realm, I realized how my own poor habits (such as not eating properly, not getting enough rest or exercise, pushing myself to the point of exhaustion) had affected my health and body.

Too late I learned that my body was precious and vitally important for many reasons and that without it I could not even pick up a piece of paper. My earthly body had many limitations, many ailments, and had caused me much pain, but I had not realized it gave me freedom as well—the freedom to act, to do the things I chose to do, and to participate in earthly experiences.

I anguished about important things I wanted to return to earth to do or finish that I could accomplish only if I had a body. While I was alive on earth I had been unhappy about what I could not do that I had believed my body would not let me do. I had more patience for someone else's physical limitations than for my own.

On the Other Side, I saw the importance of prioritizing time and tasks in order to accomplish more and still have energy left for the next day. While I was alive on earth, I did not like wasting time, and it seemed nonproductive to rest when there was so much to be done. If I had only realized the truth about health, taking care of the body, and the wise use of time, including resting when needed, I could have enjoyed my journey through life with better health.

I became aware that there is an energy-force reserve available to draw from during life on earth. When I made withdrawals from the reservoir of energy, I needed to put lifegiving things back into it by eating the right foods, maintaining a good mental attitude, taking care of relationships by doing things for others. These were important keys to keep the body's energy reserves filled and make possible earthly enjoyment and heavenly rewards.

Are We Chained to Circumstances?

During my earth life, I had taken self-improvement classes, but I still needed more confidence. There were times I believed my timid feelings and attitudes helplessly chained me to my circumstances.

As I relived these feelings, suddenly a scene was presented to my view that was symbolic of what I had thought about and how I had felt. I saw myself lying on a bright, sandy beach flat on my back. Heavy chains across my limbs bound me tightly and held me firmly against the hot sand. Lifting my head, I could see that the oppressive chains were too strong for me to escape. As I examined them, I realized and understood what they really were—my own feelings of inadequacy. They were all the put-downs from other people, my own negative self-talk, my painful feelings of incompetence, and my perceived lack of abilities.

The chains held me so that I was hardly able to move. I wondered how I had been able to function in my life with such strong chains binding me. The situation seemed hopeless, and I felt completely unable to help myself.

Just when I was about to give in to complete despair, I felt an infusion of love from God. My mind opened to the knowledge of my true nature: I was not just another life-form, I was a child of God.

What Is the Source of True Empowerment?

My thoughts centered on that incredible Being of Love and Light who stood by my side. Feelings of empowerment, self-worth, confidence, and the unconquerable courage to be myself immediately filled me. My inferiority complex was gone. All negative thoughts suddenly disappeared, replaced with my new awareness of reality.

The limits I had put on myself came to mind, and I knew that in earth life I did not need to be chained down with feelings of inadequacy. My self-worth was not dependent on other people. I was important to God, I was one of His creations, and I knew He loved me. I realized that god is no respecter of fame or fortune. Everyone is important to Him—and to themselves.

This view and understanding filled me with gratitude and a feeling of being loved. Then I sensed a feeling of freedom. In that state of mind I moved my arm; I saw that it came up freely. Amazed, I turned to look at my other arm; it was free also. The chains I had thought were so strong were actually insubstantial and powerless to hold me. Kicking my legs, I found them free as well, and now I was completely free!

Standing, I turned and looked back at the sand where I had lain so hopelessly bound just a few moments before. The chains of self-doubt had melted; they were gone. How could this be? The chains that had hampered me all my life had lacked substance and truth. No one had unlocked them, no one pulled them away from me, yet they now had no power over me. Only one thing made the difference between freedom and captivity: knowledge of my importance to God and to myself.

No person had unlocked my chains because no other person had the power to do so. The only power they had ever had was the power of my belief in them. They had seemed and felt so real, but they were not real—they were of my own making. They were a hoax, a trick I had played on myself. But no mental chains were strong enough to bind me when I realized that I was a child of God and had great personal power.

Although I didn't realize it, I always had the power to stand and walk away from my chains of self-doubt and low self-esteem. I had within me the power to dispel the dark untruths I had believed about myself throughout my life. The knowledge of my true nature turned on the light in my inner self and illuminated my path to freedom.

When I thought back on the many books I had read and courses I had taken that I had thought were fantastic, now they all seemed trivial. All the books and courses in the world were nothing when compared with the knowledge and confidence I gained when I actually realized I was a child of God.

How Does the Mind Affect the Soul?

While on the Other Side, I learned that the mind was like a powerful computer that needed to be constantly cared for with proper input. Otherwise, its product would be of poor quality—and that product is who we are.

Vividly I realized how important it was to avoid self-disparaging thoughts that would produce unwanted results. When allowed to stay in my mind, such thoughts had formed the chains that pulled me down and hindered my growth.

I realized that my mind was powerful, but it was also my servant, a part of my earthly body given to me to use wisely. I was in charge. I could have taken command of my thinking and my attitudes. I could have worked at keeping my mind on things I wanted instead of on things I worried about. On earth, I could have reprogrammed my thinking—because I was a child of God.

Self-worth and personal power, I learned, are not a result of looking or acting a certain way or achieving a certain amount. They come from knowing and remembering the truth: I am a child of God.

Is There Anything Before Life on Earth?

Suddenly the scenes in my life review were gone and scenes of my premortal life came into view. I was aware that I was part of a large group of enthusiastic supporters of the planned earth life. Immediately I knew I was not born on earth simply by chance. There were reasons— eternal purposes—for everything. I knew about the earth's creation and had a great love for it.

Everything was designed to fit together and function in harmony, and I observed that each part has a reason for being; each part supports all other parts by its existence—even insects. Things I had taken for granted or thought of as insignificant now had new importance. All things, I now knew, are significant and necessary to help the earth be whole and complete.

For example, water—an everyday substance—is important in every aspect of life on earth. Next, I knew the importance of trees that purify the air, filtering it and creating oxygen. I was never fond of trees and vegetation before. My favorite landscaping would have been almost exclusively rocks.

That changed when I found out how important trees are and how dependent everything is on everything else. Trees, vegetation, and seeds took on a new significance for me. How gloriously everything functioned; how marvelously it was created! I had a new respect and appreciation for all of God's creations. The love I had for earth was tremendous. It was incredibly important to me as I realized the significance of it in the plan and miracle of creation.

In the premortal world, I saw that it was earth life that would allow me the opportunity to have a mortal body and mortal experiences. My understanding increased as I realized why our memories of premortal life have to be hidden with an earthly veil of forgetfulness: so that we can gain wisdom—learn, develop mentally and spiritually, find joy through obedience, and become more loving, charitable, and forgiving. Also, I realized that I could not have functioned properly on earth if I had remembered the joy of being engulfed in Godly love. The longing would have been so great to be back in His presence that I could not have withstood the pain.

Did I Choose to Come to Earth?

When I was on the Other Side, I wondered about life before birth and whether I had wanted to be born or had any choice about it. My question was answered profoundly in these quick glimpses of premortality. I distinctly remembered with a burst of happiness some of the excitement I had felt about coming to earth. I knew I was not alone in this excitement; all of us were eager to participate in this plan. We were not lukewarm about this; we were exuberant. With this realization and refreshing of my memory, I felt repentant for having wondered whether I had wanted to be born—the answer was so obviously yes.

Does Each of Us Have a Purpose?

My remembrance of the premortal world while on the Other Side reawakened my feelings and knowledge about the wonders connected with being born, having a body, and being part of this eternal plan. With a bright awareness, I recalled that I wanted to help make the earth a better place for those who would come after me and be part of the whole.

My birth on earth was for a purpose, something that I accepted and wanted to accomplish. I wanted to be part of the group who were creating benefits for others in the world. I knew that each choice made on earth can have far-reaching effects. Every person and every choice matters more than we can realize at the time.

I was amazed at what I was shown and what I learned from glimpses of premortal life, scenes of the spirit world, and revelations of knowledge that were impressed upon my consciousness. The events in premortality and earth life fit together only when viewed from the Other Side.

The additional knowledge was given to me that the earth is for all of God's children, and the responsibility for it belongs to all of us. However, many of those who come to earth do not realize or care about its importance. Knowing that the earth was being fouled by some for whom it was created, whose lives depended on it, caused me to feel great sadness.

Does God Care How We Treat the Defenseless—Including Animals?

It was painful to observe those who mistreat other people under their care, including helpless children and the elderly. Their pain when confronted with their own actions will be worse than the pain that they inflicted.

Thoughts came to my mind of those who, regrettably, discount the intelligence, emotions, and pain of animals—and any creatures on earth—sometimes because they don't care and sometimes because they don't realize the eternal nature of God's creations. I knew that many people on earth greatly underestimate how much God cares about His animals and other creatures and how people treat them. It was sad that many who had great potential fell short of their potential in their treatment of their families, others, and defenseless creatures.

It was exciting, however, to learn of the tremendous joy awaiting those who accept their challenges and make it through them while striving to keep God's commandments—they then reap their earned rewards. I had an overwhelming desire to be among the group on earth who serve Him and do His will.

However, many of my own free-will choices while I was alive on earth had brought me feelings of remorse instead.

Is There a Reason We Have the Parents We Do?

My life review continued, and my attention focused on scenes with my mother. I became aware of thoughts I'd had on earth, such as, "Why didn't I have someone else as my mother or my father?" I heard my thoughts: "My life would have been so much better if I had had different parents. I could have accomplished so much more." It was as though those thoughts were visible around me. I tried to escape from them, but I could not.

Just as suddenly, other things were in my view and I knew that I had chosen my mother, although I wasn't told this was the case for everyone else. I had wanted to be her daughter, not for the things she could do for me on earth but for what I could do for her. She needed me!

She was a special, precious person who needed my help to make it through her journey of earth life. In her own way, she was hurting as much as I had been.

Our life together had been filled with contention and arguments over what was truth and who was right. We had often used words that hurt each other, and our relationship had been extremely frustrating for both of us. It seemed we were always angry with each other.

For years I had longed to hear her tell me she loved me and that she was sorry about my unhappy childhood. I wanted her to accept me, but I felt I could never please her. We argued over big things and little things. A poem came to mind that I had written when I was a teenager expressing my mistaken feelings about being right. The poem reads:

Oh, Mother, dear, I sadly fear
that until we die
we will continue to try
to argue and fight
to prove who is right
although we both know, I am.

Erroneously, I had believed that finding out who was "right" would cure almost any situation. I had falsely believed that a vigorous pursuit of justice in all things was essential, as if it would automatically stop wrongful actions as soon as "truth" was discovered. The stark reality of how false this notion was became clear to me. I discovered how wrong I was to quarrel about being right, and I saw that people all believe, or like to think, that they're right.

Who was right or wrong, whether or not she was sorry, or whether she told me she loved me were no longer concerns. Oh, how my feelings for my mother and my understanding of her changed! No longer did I feel compelled to have her say or do something to show that she loved me. I felt her feelings and I knew of her love for me.

My awareness exploded with the information and reality of how much my mother needed me. My love for her blossomed, and I realized her heartaches and life's trials. I missed her in this spiritual sphere, and I wanted to help her and talk to her; I was saddened and frustrated that I could not. As I realized this, my feelings of remorse intensified. I had let us both down. Also, I knew that she had a difficult time telling me she loved me and she needed me to tell her I loved her.

The foolishness and futility of bickering and

fighting with anyone was impressed upon me. I was very sorry for wasting irreplaceable time in senseless arguing about happenings, situations, opinions, and who was right. My sorrow was extreme for every harsh or sharp word I had ever spoken to anyone, especially family members.

Also, I saw that people watch and learn from each other and repeat each other's actions and mistakes. It became clear to me how everyone's actions influence the lives of countless others.

New scenes quickly came to my view containing additional important messages for me. I saw a mother teaching her daughter to clean a floor thoroughly. Her voice was sweet as she approvingly said, "The floor looks nice and clean, but that corner could look better and needs to be redone." The mother's words conveyed her love and acceptance and did not make the girl feel rejected but motivated her to improve her skills. I understood that the mother's object was not only to get the floor clean but to instill confidence in her child and to teach her good work habits for life.

Again, the scene before me changed swiftly, and I saw another mother belittling her child for not doing the chores according to her standards. The mother grabbed the cleaning cloth from her daughter and said in a sharp tone, "Why do I have to do everything myself? You are so clumsy, you can't do anything right." Then she did the task herself. I saw the young child cringe as she developed habitual feelings of inferiority and depression that would lead her toward giving up.

I became aware that the ultimate goal in teaching children is to help them learn and mature so that they can succeed without being supervised. They need a safe family environment in order to gain wisdom, confidence, and the experience of doing things on their own. They need an inner desire to do things correctly, not because they are being watched or because someone makes them perform their tasks to an acceptable standard.

Are My Children Really Mine?

This was an enlightening revelation for me. I wanted to cry out to my children—to apologize for the times I was impatient with them as they went through their learning experiences during childhood. Then I also knew that my children were actually God's children entrusted to my care. From this perspective, I understood that problems as I was raising them were really opportunities for us to learn some of life's valuable lessons, such as the connection between choices and consequences.

I had always loved my children, but now I had gained a vivid new understanding of how extremely important and precious they were. Also, I missed them in this sphere and I longed to be able to talk to them. I wanted to tell them about things they could do on earth that would help them prepare for their journey to the Other Side.

Now scenes from the priceless child-rearing years passed rapidly for my review. The swift passage of the time I had with my children brought the distinct realization that my best opportunities for teaching them were gone—in fact, all opportunities to be with them or to teach them on earth were gone.

When I was alive on earth, I had seen a wall plaque with a saying on it: "Life was what happened while I was busy with other plans." I was struck in this spiritual realm with the actuality of that statement. Before I realized it, those brief childhood times while my children's questioning minds were so open and accepting of ideas had passed, never to be recaptured.

I looked back over the years when my children were small, with their minds absorbing my philosophies and attitudes as they matured. I heard words I had said many times as they were growing up, and winced: "Who's at fault? Tell the truth—what happened here? We have to be fair about this. You are wrong."

Those parenting phrases seemed normal; they were ones I had often heard in my own childhood, and so I repeated them as a parent. I wanted to raise my children to seek fairness and justice. That was how I had been raised and how my mother had been raised.

The scenes I viewed while I was on the Other Side revealed to me the error of seeking "truth" and "fairness" over teaching forgiveness and tolerance. Being right or establishing fault faded into insignificance compared to being concerned about feelings, building character, and developing self-esteem while children are young and most open to training.

Again, once I understood this lesson, I saw a montage of scenes. I felt the feelings of small children as they took harsh verbal attacks from parents locked into patterns of false child-rearing notions that went back several generations, including put-downs and words that battered self-images, words that could hurt like a blow from a fist.

I saw parents yelling at their children, parents who in frustration and anger falsely believed they were reacting normally to their situations. The children absorbed like little sponges the tone of their parents' voices and the tension around them. Like little tape recorders, they were recording in their minds the words they heard their parents use.

Then I saw those same children as adults with their own children. It was as though someone hit the playback button on their mental tape recorders. They were using their parents' impatient and ineffective responses word for word. They were parenting the way they had been taught, following their parents' unsuccessful example.

Then my own children came into my view, and I knew how precious and important they were as part of my life. Each child had been like a jewel I was given on earth to care for, lovingly polish, and help develop its special radiance. I loved them very much and wanted to communicate with them. My love and concern for them were infinitely more now than while I was with them in earth life. I had had no idea that the "spiritual sphere" was this way. I wanted to go back to earth to warn them not to repeat the mistakes I had made.

Suddenly my feelings of remorse in regard to my lack of parenting skills ceased. Wait! I thought defensively, I had not been given an "owner's manual" when I had my first child, nor had my mother. I was doing the best I knew how, and so had my mother, and so had her parents. We believed we were doing right at the time. In reality, we were functioning at our own level of growth, just as everyone does.

Are Children Trapped in Their Parents' Patterns?

I also realized that people can break free of undesirable teachings and habits, including undesired family patterns. It is not easy, yet it can be done with the help of the Creator through the power of prayer and a person's own self-determination. My excuses continued to melt in the bright light of truth.

The perspectives I gained about all the members of my family cast a new light of understanding on the importance of every pattern handed down from one generation to another. I wanted to change many of the ones that were being handed down to my posterity—but now I could not.

Are There Angels?

As soon as I grasped the meaning of these scenes, I found myself traveling through time and space, through a star-filled blackness. Suddenly, as though I had been drawn into a hologram, a three-dimensional scene, I saw generations of parents and children acting out their daily routines.

Watching, I was aware of the positive and negative consequences of their parenting patterns and the habits that were affecting their lives. Knowledge penetrated my being of the repercussions of these patterns and family traditions as they had been passed to me and I had passed them on to my children.

The Being of Love and Light was just a few feet from me as I viewed these scenes, and I knew that without his power I couldn't have seen any of this.

Knowledge about the people I was seeing continued to flash into my mind, and I somehow knew that some of them were future generations of my own family. As I saw untrue ideas and negative patterns passed on and on to generations of my descendants, I had a great desire to return to earth and stop that cycle.

But the Being of Love and Light had more to show me.

I seemed to be floating in and out of different scenes, and in one I saw a beautiful young woman with lovely dark hair and deep blue eyes. She was more substantial than the figures below, and I couldn't stop staring at her, feeling somehow drawn to her. As our eyes met, she smiled and held out her arms toward me. But then she paused, and with her arms still outstretched she said, "I've waited so long." Putting her arms down, she turned and disappeared from the hologram. Only much later was I to learn who she was.

What Is the Most Important Thing in Life?

I was struck with the knowledge of how important the family and home life are—more important than anything else. Any other success is temporary. I knew that all the success the world has to offer is meaningless beside nurturing the family well.

Even though I had been away from my family largely because of poor health, I knew we could have spent more quality time together. If I had been able to set a better example for them by being more empathetic, loving, and nurturing, rather than seeking "fairness" to settle sibling disputes, it would have strengthened family relationships.

With this awareness, as I looked at all these precious ones, I wanted to hide from them. I didn't want to admit who I was or that part of the problems they would have on earth stemmed from me and what I had or had not done. I knew now that all actions, large and small, good and bad, have eternal consequences.

As soon as I had that thought, I recalled Kristy, my granddaughter, sitting quietly at my home and playing a silly game that occupied much of her free time. I re-heard the soft "ping, ping, ping" when she scored points as she played the game over and over. Her concentration was intense. I had a burning feeling that there were other things she needed to do and learn, things that would help her in her mortal development.

Spending so much time playing that unproductive game was creating a void in her development. Instead, she should be learning things she could pass on to her posterity. She had waited a long time for her opportunity to have a mortal body, and her precious time was being squandered in front of a video screen I had purchased for her and taught her how to use. I wanted to return to earth life and hide that game.

Looking at my posterity all around me, I sadly realized that my lack of child-rearing skills would contribute to some of the unhappiness they would have when they went to earth. Challenges resulting from my inadequacy would ricochet through time. I knew of some of the trials they would go through in their lives; troubles caused by lack of knowledge that I failed to teach my children, and that they in turn failed to teach theirs, and so on.

There were things they would not learn on earth that would have greatly benefited them. I saw that my posterity could trace this lack of knowledge for generations, back to my children, to me, to my mother, to my ancestors. During my earth life, I had never thought of these things, but in the spirit world, they were apparent.

My anguish intensified as I understood the far-reaching effects of not helping my granddaughter learn more worthwhile things. Kristy was losing precious growing experiences that would mean some lost eternal rewards that she might otherwise have gained as she taught her posterity, my posterity.

I saw that gaining wisdom and overcoming

problems are some of the grand keys God gives us to unlock our own happiness and the growth and happiness of our posterity and those around us. I saw how loving parenting skills would help all concerned. Also, I realized the importance of believing that situations and relationships can improve and then working to better things rather than being quick to judge and give up on a family member.

As I mingled with angels and those whom I knew were to be my posterity, my understanding was opened and I knew that these parenting skills were some of the important lessons that were to be learned in the school of life.

Why Are We All So Different? Is There a Purpose for Diversity?

Suddenly I was again whirling through time and space. My view opened to new scenes, and I saw the history of the world unfold on a huge panoramic screen. Life seemed like a puzzle with pieces falling into place. It was so exhilarating! I thought of how people on earth think programs on TV or in movies are exciting, but they pale when compared to the history of our own fascinating world.

I had heard a lot of negative things about the world and its history, but just as in my own day, in years past much good had gone unnoticed. It probably always would until everything is known on the Other Side.

I saw that fashions and standards of beauty changed over the years. My attention focused on a scene where I saw a fairly large, portly woman who was considered a true beauty in her time. She was posing semi-nude for a painting.

Instantly, I knew that she felt proud to be posing for this painting but there would come a time when she would regret it. At this moment, however, she was proud of herself, her beauty, and her roly-poly figure. I chuckled when I thought of all the poor thin women of her day who envied her her full figure. They disliked their looks and felt lacking in feminine beauty because their bodies did not match their time period's standard of loveliness when it was fashionable to be plump.

Is It a Sin to Be Overweight?

The beauty standard in my time was almost the exact opposite. I learned that the fat-or-thin question was a passing fad that changed with time and was not important in Heaven. With stark realization, I knew that while on earth we may be teased or belittled if our size or looks do not match the current standard of beauty. However, the standards by which we are judged on earth change often and are not of lasting significance.

I knew that a healthy body at an ideal weight for each person's frame (not thin) would become fashionable. I was surprised to learn this about weight; it was such a big issue during my lifetime. I was surprised to learn that being overweight did not reap ridicule on the Other Side as it does in earth life. However, there is obvious wisdom in eating right.

Glimpses were shown me of men and women who desired to be in style and in vogue with fashions that changed with the whims of their time. I knew that they sacrificed important things in their lives for fancy clothes, jewelry, and other material things, to stay at the height of whatever was considered the "in thing" at the time. It seemed silly to me from my Other Side viewpoint, and I learned how important it was to keep a balance. Priorities needed to be grounded by an eternal perspective of heavenly treasures that did not wear out or go out of style.

As the years passed and styles changed, I saw that apparel that had been so important lost its appeal as the newest or latest fashion was desired instead. After people who had been caught up in fashion trends passed on to the Other Side, they became aware of the foolishness of their behavior. They were disappointed in themselves for wasting their time and resources on frivolous earthly things when they found out that people and family were so much more important than things.

Abruptly, my view of the scenes and the panorama of the history of earth ended, and the spirit world was again revealed. I was surprised as I realized more about God's ever-present and observable love. Feeling His love was glorious and beautiful—a beauty that encompassed everything and everyone in my view.

Does Beauty Really Come from Within?

It is difficult to describe the beauty of the people I saw and felt in the spiritual sphere. It was incredible. I am not talking about outer beauty, but a loveliness that came from deep within and enhanced physical features.

This inner radiance had nothing to do with

age. In fact, age itself was interesting; it seemed to me that everyone I saw or of whom I was aware was at their ideal age, although there were those who seemed older and those who seemed younger. I do not believe those who appeared older were actually older spirits; perhaps they looked that way for my view.

Were People in the Spirit World All Young and Beautiful?

In earth life, youth and beauty had seemed so connected. On the Other Side, I was surprised that two spirits who were among the most attractive were a man and a woman who looked older to me. Their faces were creased and lined with wrinkles, and I realized that each of their wrinkles was a visual testament of the lives they had led in mortality.

My understanding was opened to this new thought, and I became aware of the sorrows and trials this man and woman had withstood in life. Each wrinkle seemed to be a badge of valor that stood for their righteous concerns, a crisis, or an ongoing struggle they had successfully weathered. Each line seemed to tell a story; every action, every thought, pain, and concern were known. They were beautiful people because of their mercy, compassion, patience, and love for others. I was awed because I had never considered wrinkles or lines in the face to be attractive, but they were to me now, as I understood what these people had gone through, and knew of their tears and pleas to God for mercy and help for others.

Then I began noticing other faces more carefully. There were some who were marred by the lines in their faces. Since every action and thought was known, I knew that many of these lines had been formed by frowning, scowling, excessive anger, and mean-spiritedness. Their faces reflected their former enjoyment of gloating, hurting, and taking advantage of others while on earth. These choices were now causing them anguish and sorrow.

What a contrast! Suddenly I understood a great truth about beauty. On earth, I believed beauty came from youth and flawless features. In the spirit world, it became obvious that beauty is created from loving, caring, charitable thinking and actions—by endurance through trials with good attitudes. It came from within and was manifested in the outer appearance.

I saw many who had been considered plain and homely on earth accepted among the most lovely, according to the way they had conducted themselves while in mortality. I saw that those who had an illusion of beauty while in mortality would be seen by eyes of new understanding on the Other Side. They would be perceived from every angle. They had a special radiance if they had conducted themselves well while in their earthly life.

My concept of beauty was greatly expanded to include my view of everyone as a whole person with the inner self and outer beauty radiating a loving countenance, or lack of it. Looks from an earthly perspective were insignificant in the afterlife.

I received the marvelous knowledge that all good thoughts and deeds are eventually rewarded and add to a person's eternal, radiating countenance.

Are the Words We Speak and Write Ever Lost?

On the Other Side, words are not required for clear understanding because all thoughts and intentions are known and understood with clarity.

Words that have been spoken, however, do not just disappear into the air; they remain and can be tuned in to and understood. I believe I could have heard anything from the Beatitudes to the Gettysburg Address just as if I were there when they were first uttered. All words are still present if the time is right to tune in to them. As I realized that all thoughts, words, and deeds are waiting for review on the Other Side, I wished I could call back all the harsh words I had spoken.

I wanted to communicate to my posterity. I realized it would have been valuable to have left them a written account of what I had learned during earth life. But now I couldn't—I didn't have my body anymore.

In the spiritual·sphere, I saw and felt the importance of writing in diaries or journals and keeping track of family history. I realized keenly that as a person grows and develops in life, it is important to leave a written account of the lessons we learn along the way so that others who follow may benefit from our experiences. I understood the importance of learning from the personal experiences of others.

The difficulty and yet the importance of conveying to posterity the lessons learned during earth life were profoundly impressed upon my mind! Also, I knew that journals and family history accounts could be visible gifts of love for posterity to read. Through them, people could get to know their ancestors and have an understanding of who they were and what they believed.

Family history and journals could make it possible for posterity to continue worthwhile traditions, develop their own family traditions, and have a better chance to avoid pitfalls that may have plagued other family members before them.

During earth life, I had occasionally written in journals, but I didn't keep it up. I had many excuses and believed my journals would not be interesting to anyone. I now saw that someday some of my posterity—my children's children and their children—would be interested in reading my journals and their family history. They would want to know about me, their great-great-grandmother, who had lived before them during earth life.

Previously, I had thought of myself as a daughter, granddaughter, and great-granddaughter, but now I realized I would also be a great-grandmother and a great-great-grandmother, and so on. I had never really thought about posterity, other than my grandchildren who were already born, until I had this glimpse of them. Then I knew the importance of leaving them a written account of their family history. I had an overwhelming desire to communicate to them, to let them know that I cared.

As I thought of the love and concern I had for my previously unknown future family members, they did not seem too distant or too many to know and love. Love is limitless and has no bounds.

Thinking about the importance of family journals, I knew that the tone of the messages within them needed to be positive and upbeat—not writings that might hurt or embarrass another person or things that someone might decide to tear up and throw away. They needed to be uplifting, yet true.

It became evident how much power there is in saying good things about others and keeping a record of the highlights of life, yet not disregarding challenges or pitfalls. I realized the need of emphasizing messages such as "keep on keeping on," of looking for blessings and recording miracles. It was also important to keep the writings focused on overcoming and learning so that posterity could look back and grow from what was shared with them.

There was great value, I now knew, in writing and sharing messages of hope and encouragement—nuggets of knowledge and wisdom learned from the journey of life.

Some people have suggested writing down bad experiences, even venomous words and the worst of feelings; but for every action, even writing down feelings, there is absolutely a reaction. Forgiving, letting go, and loving unconditionally are worthwhile thoughts and actions that will be multiplied for the good of all concerned, especially when recording events and feelings in journals. Words are powerful!

Are There Heavenly Stress Reducers?

My thoughts expanded with an increased awareness of many people living on earth during my lifetime and how they suffered under burdens of stress unique to our period of the world's ongoing history. I became aware of many things that could decrease stress, such as overcoming negative patterns of reacting to other people with anger and following wise counsel as taught in Scriptures, such as "judge not that ye be not judged." I knew that the more scriptural teachings were followed, the more stress would be relieved.

I also knew that during earth life, being empathetic and less easily offended adds to peace of mind and will extend to the Other Side.

Is Time in a Different Dimension on the Other Side?

Everything I saw over there was communicated to me with clear understanding. Some scenes were separate from others and some were connected, although it was as if they were all still present. Time has a different dimension in the spiritual realm. Describing it as the third dimension seems inadequate; a fourth dimension may be a more accurate description.

The scenes continued and I realized how advanced the earth's current period of history is, technologically and otherwise. My view did not end with the past or present; the panorama continued into the future. I recall that it seemed humorous to me that I once thought the present was so advanced, because it is still in the "Dark Ages" compared to what will be forthcoming in the future.

I was truly inspired to realize how earth knowledge and technology will continue to advance and expand. For instance, great discoveries and improvements will be made in what is considered "conventional" medical treatments. Alternate fields of healing will be more accepted and there will be faster, more accurate diagnostic techniques and treatments. Other technological advances, I learned, would dwarf what I knew during my earth life.

My feelings about so many things were changed from seeing history happen. Again, it was like seeing puzzle pieces that had been randomly scattered finally fit together.

Do Caring Relationships End at Death?

It was impressed upon me that heavenly, caring relationships begin on earth and do not end at death. In fact, they are stronger and even more special on the Other Side.

I observed both men and women there, and I was aware that we maintain the same gender as in life. I remained me—a woman and a mother who greatly cared about her family, a daughter concerned about her mother. I knew that relationships of family and friends continue and we will be reunited with our loved ones who have passed on.

Now I knew that friendship, companionship, and the relationships between men and women are special—more than I had ever realized before.

My thoughts were immediately filled with the all-encompassing love from the Being of Light. As I rejoiced and felt encircled in His love, I knew that God's love was so great it dissolved all my feelings that I was unloved.

I experienced a sharp awareness of an increased love and caring for my family and friends. My concern wasn't only for those people with whom I now felt ties, but also for people I had hardly known and those I had not previously known who were connected to me.

Is It Possible to Have a "Happy Homecoming" When We Die?

I became aware of many of my ancestors, including some I had heard about as a child. The knowledge came to me that if we have met the challenges in life and then died (that is, if our arrival on the Other Side is not the result of our own misguided actions), we are received in an attitude of homecoming. We are greeted with a great outpouring of love from those on the Other Side who have been anxiously watching and who have been eager for us to succeed on earth in our mortal school. Ancestors and posterity are concerned for our success during our earth life and exist in a sphere close to us even though we cannot see them with our mortal eyes. Our ancestors love and care for us and we love them. We are important to each other.

However, those who do something to cause their own death—commit suicide or give up and regrettably will themselves to die when it's not their time, as I did—may have feelings of real sadness for blessings that were lost by their own actions. Also, there may be a turning away of loved ones, posterity and ancestors whom we let down. Especially ancestors who had endured difficulties, suffered, and sacrificed for their posterity may turn away rather than welcome someone's untimely arrival on the Other Side.

Do Our Ancestors Know and Care About Us?

There were no greater supporters, I realized, than my ancestors who had paved my way with their actions and their very lives. I remember that there were many—some were dressed in angelic white robes, others in clothing that seemed appropriate for differing periods of history. I was aware that they could appear to me in different attire if it would help my understanding.

Their manner of dress was not impressed on my mind as vividly as was my discomfort in being with them; I wanted to retreat from their presence. Their exact words were not clear, but I understood that they wanted to convey definite messages of love and concern. They were sad that I had given up. I knew that most of them had endured many more physical hardships than I had faced on earth and yet they did not give up. Knowing this, I felt great sorrow that I had not done better with my earth time. These feelings of regret were woven like threads through my entire experience on the Other Side.

My ancestors cared about the decisions I made, my actions, and my happiness. Their attitudes could best be described as those of mental and spiritual cheerleaders. I learned that there are many people interested in each of us—more than I ever imagined. As I realized my importance to them, I knew how disappointed they were when I cheated myself by willing myself to die instead of making the most of my opportunities.

While I was on the Other Side, I was aware that when I was alive on earth and influenced by anger, false pride, or sin, I repelled rather than attracted special spiritual blessings. I saw that when I was tempted to give up on life, to think and act contrary to God's laws, I was vulnerable to influence by spirits who desired my failure, depression, and sadness. Those dark spirits found satisfaction when I strayed from my goals in life and forfeited peace of mind on the Other Side. I knew they were real and as desirous of my failure as my spiritual and ancestral cheerleaders were of my success.

How Can We Get Rid of the Influence of Dark Spirits?

The realization came to me that these darker spirits were unable to reach me when I chose positive, uplifting thoughts and activities—especially when I prayed, or read the Scriptures and pondered their spiritual messages! I had my freedom to choose what to think and what to do, and God was there to help me with my choices. Dark spirits have limitations and could influence my thoughts only if I permitted them to.

Knowing that thoughts create attitudes and then produce actions, I learned the importance of controlling thoughts. I recognized wrongful patterns such as envy, anger, and hurtful actions for what they had been—dangers to my lasting happiness.

As I wondered how to combat the efforts of dark spirits, I thought about comparing a cleansing shower with reading and pondering the Scriptures. Scripture study was like a spiritual shower because it caused the dark spirits to disappear; they recoiled in the presence of Godly things. I could have felt spiritually clean and more receptive to inspiration by studying great eternal truths, more capable of living a Godlike life, and more able to take part in God's grand plan.

It was now clear that there are many truths and answers in Scriptures and other great books of holy writings that could have given me a more righteous perspective and a more abundant life. The path of life for lasting peace is detailed there. For example, in the wisdom contained in the Beatitudes and in Scripture, "Inasmuch as ye have done it unto one of the least of these, my brethren, ye have done it unto me [God]. (St. Matthew 25:40 KJV).

However, I realized that these books could not give guidance if they were not read! I knew that reading them, studying them prayerfully, and pondering them, allows knowledge to enter the mind and opens the channel of inspiration and understanding for a higher way of living that causes dark spirits to flee. Now I understood how literally true, yet understated the Holy Scriptures are.

As I understood the wisdom and eternal truth of these writings, and how powerful they were, all the thousands of books written to help everyone come to the same conclusions seemed irrelevant. Most of them would not be necessary if Scriptures were really studied, understood, and applied in our lives. However, I also realized that the myriad of books and self-improvement courses can be stepping-stones leading to better understanding and application of the teachings of the Scriptures and other great books—knowledge of eternal truths helps us overcome the stumbling blocks in the journey of life.

Is It Possible to Gain Lasting Peace of Mind?

It was surprising to learn how much God loves and appreciates the sincere and devout of all faiths who seek to better themselves and aid humanity. The love of God abounds for all—He is no respecter of persons, of one over another. Never before had I felt so connected with all people and all religions as I did when I realized the extent of His love. He has such rich rewards waiting for those who sincerely strive to follow Him.

I wondered why there were so many religions on earth, and I wondered about the greatly varying teachings, scriptures, and interpretations of them. It was shown to me that some teachings in different religions in the world are nearer to God's truths than others. Those that are closest are generally found in some form in all religions; for example, treating others as we would have them treat us. I was keenly aware that we are all at our own level of spiritual beliefs and at our own level of ability to live by religious teachings. I had a bright awareness that God is pleased with all those who strive for righteousness.

As people fervently and sincerely seek to know the truth and to live God's laws, He is pleased, and their spiritual selves are expanded. They become capable of receiving more inspiration, knowledge, and truth; they reap blessings. I knew that the more people apply the knowledge and inspiration they are given, the more they can receive.

I was also shown that there were many people who were complacent and unwisely satisfied with what they believe. Yet I was aware that there were vast numbers of people sincerely striving to gain answers to life's questions and knowledge of eternal truths. Driven by a great hunger and thirst for righteousness, they sample the teachings of many religions of the world. Seeking to drink from a "living well," they rightly search until they find the religion that gives them divine guidance and inner peace.

These sincere people look for the religion that they believe is right for them and that fulfills their quest for knowledge about their own true purpose for living.

Is Anything Too Small for God's Concern?

My wonderment continued as I realized how all-knowing God is. No care or problem is too small for Him to know everything about it.

I realized that God offers a peace beyond comprehension or description, an eternal peace of mind! I had never even imagined that God was so all-knowing. As my understanding was opened, I knew that He is fully aware of everyone's problems, temptations, and sorrows. He is aware of sincerity, righteous sacrifices, and the intent of each heart as His children strive to live by His commandments.

My being was filled with love and appreciation for the sincere believers of all the world's religions. I understood that God's holy words offer a lasting peace beyond worldly description for all. The greatest and most lasting peace of mind for earth life and the Other Side is offered to all humanity by God.

How Can We Connect to Heavenly Power?

Next, I saw and became aware of many aspects of prayer and how important it is to pray. Learning that prayer truly is a conversation with God, I realized that He wanted to hear from me and to communicate with me. I then knew the importance of expressing gratitude and appreciation for all my blessings—from small things to great miracles.

Feeling remorseful that I had taken for granted many special blessings, I now saw my life in its proper perspective. I knew that electricity was powerful and capable of mighty accomplishments when something is connected to it. But I saw that being connected to heavenly power in prayer is an infinitely greater power, which draws from a "heavenly treasury." I knew that miracles are possible and happen much more frequently than acknowledged on earth.

During my earth life, I had not adequately realized this amazing source of power. Many times I prayed from habit or because I needed something in particular. But at this point, I saw prayer, silent and spoken, as a two-way communication with someone I loved and respected, who loved me and had the power to bless me for my good. In my life review, I saw that many of my prayers had been granted, and I felt remorse that I had not recognized and expressed appreciation for my blessings.

Knowledge was given to me about "No" answers to prayers and how they had been for my benefit. Also, I more fully realized the great importance of doing what I could with what I had and appreciating it, rather than concentrating on and lamenting over what I did not have.

My mind was quickened with the knowledge that there were answers to prayers and blessings I had received where I had falsely given the credit to "coincidence" instead of giving thanks to God in all things.

Why Do You Visualize a Personal God?

Knowledge was given to me about the importance of praying regularly and thinking of God as a person. There were times when I used to pray and my mind would wander because I did not have a clear understanding or a mental picture of God. I was thrilled to know that He is an actual Being who has feelings and that He loves me. This was not just some cloud I was speaking to when I knelt in prayer. I discovered He is much more knowledgeable, understanding, and loving than any person I could ever imagine knowing.

Do We Really Receive Answers to Our Prayers?

My awareness was opened to some of the many things involved in receiving answers to prayers, such as the sincerity of mind and heart and the readiness of the person to receive the help asked for. Sometimes an answer to a prayer to have a burden removed comes in the form of strength to carry it rather than a miracle to take it away.

Also, I saw the definite connection between the likelihood of receiving mercy and help requested to the mercy and help the person praying has given others. Knowledge was given me that God usually uses willing people to answer the prayers of others. I became aware that our prayers are more apt to be answered when we ask and respond positively to the questions "Whose burden could I lighten today as I ask God to help ease mine? Who is waiting to hear from me? With wisdom, whose pain could I ease with loving words or deeds so I could then ask with a clear conscience for my prayer to be answered?"

God is keenly aware of everyone's prayers. It is unproductive to ask Him to answer our prayers when we deliberately ignore the needs of those we ought to be mindful of—especially elderly parents and grandparents who wait to hear or need help from children and loved ones.

Scenes came to my mind of people on earth who were preoccupied with their babies and other children to the extent that they neglected aging parents and grandparents who had expended their time, strength, and means to care for them when they were young.

As the years rolled by, some of the elderly parents in the scenes I viewed became so weak that they were no longer able to care for themselves. They needed attention from their children and grandchildren. Because they felt lost and forgotten, they gave up and simply waited to die. What a difference a visit, a phone call, or a card would have made to them. They waited day after day, with no contact from even their closest loved ones—those to whom they had given their own time and resources.

Watching and hearing older parents and grandparents praying and asking God to ease their burdens and loneliness made me feel great sadness for all concerned. I was aware that many promptings to their children to make those requested calls or visits were sadly unheeded. Yet, the children and grandchildren were asking God to answer their own prayers while they remained oblivious to those whose prayers they could so easily answer.

How Can I Hear the Whisperings of the Spirit?

I learned that while praying to God, expressing gratitude, and asking for blessings, it is also very important to pause and take time to listen to promptings that may come as whisperings from the Holy Spirit. Promptings may be blocked by becoming too caught up in "asking." Only when we take time to listen can we receive the inspiration, promptings, and guidance that bring peace beyond measure.

Continually asking for blessings, I realized, without giving sincere thanks, is like a child asking a parent for more and more without taking time to give thanks and appreciation for what has already been received. As earthly parents want to be appreciated, so does God.

PART THREE

☙❧

*Each Day We Are Given
a Second Chance—What We Do
with It Is Up to Us*

Vividly aware of how my decisions and actions could so personally affect the lives of others and myself, I longed for the chance to come back and make right what I could—to progress and grow through life and not run from it. I wanted to come back and change whatever ill effects my death would cause others and to use my earth time more effectively.

Although I had not actually committed suicide, I had completely surrendered my life, willing myself to die, and God had granted my desire. Now, in this sphere, the implications of my choices were clear. Starkly apparent were things that I wanted to do on earth that I had not done yet could have done. Thoughts of my family came again to my mind, and I wanted to tell them what I had learned about the Other Side.

Also, I wanted to share with others who were seeking hope the heavenly answers to problems on earth that I had discovered. I wanted to shout the real value of life on earth and the foolishness of trying to cut life short to escape problems and physical discomfort.

When I saw things in the proper perspective, I wanted to live, even in an aching, mortal body. Every part of my mind, heart, and spirit begged to have another chance to go back to the earthly sphere. Feelings of "if only" were tormenting me.

In the spiritual sphere, I was free from physical pain for the first time in many long years, yet the emotional anguish I was feeling was many times worse than the physical pain I'd had when I was alive. I wanted to escape this spiritual misery even more than I had wanted to escape my physical pain.

Unhappily, I felt that asking to return was useless. I had lived my life. I had had the chance to live or die and had chosen to die. I had prayed for death and here it was. It seemed futile to request another chance, yet I couldn't stop myself. The more I thought about the opportunities I had let slip past me, the more I wanted to be allowed to return.

A Gift from God

Suddenly a huge tooth appeared before me as if it were hanging in the air. It was enlarged many times, giving me views of its surfaces. It was my gold-crowned tooth, crowned at least fifteen years earlier.

During all those years I had not given that tooth any thought because it had not given me any pain. I had had a thorough dental checkup not long before this experience, and all my teeth were fine. But as information about this particular tooth was given me, I knew that it was a serious problem, and was an important part of the answer to recovering my physical health.

Just as suddenly as it had appeared, the tooth vanished and I was quickly drawn back into my body. Still leaning forward toward the inside of the tub, I stared at the bottom of the bathtub for a while, realizing that, miraculously, I was back on earth. I began trying to push myself up from the edge of the tub. Slowly I made my body move. My fingers moved; I gradually moved my hands and touched my face. I was solid, mortally alive again!

Turning my head, I noted with amazement that I could see only what was in my normal field of vision. The "everywhere at once" vision I'd had in the spirit world was gone.

At the same time, I was again aware of physical pain; I ached throughout my whole body. There were sharp pains in my arms, legs, hands, and feet, and I had very little strength. My weakness was so profound that it made gravity seem powerful and oppressive. But I didn't care. I had no desire to exchange my situation of pain and sickness for that light, floaty, pain-free existence. I was being given another chance at life!

The anguish was gone; my agony of spirit was over. Kneeling shakily and leaning on the tub, I felt the glorious thrill of once again being alive and on the earth. My pleas to return to earth life had been granted. Gratitude welled up inside of me. Joy and relief overwhelmed me. I was overjoyed to be where I was, even grateful to feel exhausted, to feel my body's pain, and to feel ill.

I tried to get back into bed and found that I couldn't walk; even crawling was difficult. The effort was exhausting because I was so weak, and my movements were slow. But all the way I kept thinking, "I can move my body. I am alive!" I didn't know how long I was on the Other Side.

Even though I was ill, I now knew that being alive was a great blessing. I was determined to stop putting limitations on my body by thinking negative thoughts about my health. My body was precious and priceless no matter what it looked like or how ill it was.

Knowing the significance of returning to earth life, though, and being thrilled that I could speak again, I said aloud, "I am back, I am really back." Tears of joy spilled down my cheeks. Then concerns struck me.

I'm back, but for how long?

How long will I be given to do the things I want to do in earth life?

How much time will I have to put into practice the perspectives that I gained?

No answer came to me. Knowing that I had no guarantees, no idea of the length of time I was being given, I knew I had to make every moment count. Being anxious to get busy living, I wanted to stand up and start right then. My weakness, though, was such that I could only lie there and contemplate how much I had learned, and how much I wanted to do.

When I felt somewhat stronger, I made my way into the family room, where Kristy's foolish video game—my gift to her—was located. Slowly, I unhooked the game from the back of the TV set, gathered up the cords and controllers, and hid them away. Then I returned to bed.

Throughout the next two weeks, I felt the odd sensation that at any time, night or day, I could step back into that other sphere, the spirit world. The knowledge I had gained was still fresh in my mind. I could call up the images I had seen at will and re-experience my visit there. Memories of the larger picture of life and of life after death impressed upon my mind that earth life is very temporary.

Although I wanted to be alive with all my heart, I did not want to lose my enlightenment, my knowledge, and the new awareness I had gained. I hoped that this bright awareness and access to the Other Side would last the rest of my life, but gradually I felt the spirit world begin to slip away. With my new knowledge, I understood that I could not continue to live on earth unless I was able to experience life's trials and temptations in a natural way, and little by little I reentered mortality and felt a part of earth life once again.

The experience I had and the scenes I had viewed, which contained symbolic, life-changing messages for me, seemed miraculous. Wanting to tell anyone who would listen, I soon told those closest to me, the people I trusted the most. My experience was sufficiently personal, though, that I was careful with whom I shared it.

The next time Kristy came to visit, she was upset that the game was gone, but being an easygoing child, she soon adjusted and began doing other, more worthwhile things. Although it wasn't easy giving up my electronic baby-sitter, it was well worth it, for I received peace of mind seeing Kristy grow mentally and spiri-tually by finding better ways of using her time.

Kristy went on to college, and there she met her future husband. They were married and now have three children, including a little girl, Jessica, who has lovely brown hair and beautiful blue eyes. She was the young woman I felt drawn to when I was in the spirit realm, who greeted me with a smile and outstretched arms. I'm grateful that I have lived to see and know on earth so many of my posterity. Hopefully they will learn what they need to from their time on earth. I certainly pray that they do.

Proof of My Visions

Among my most vivid memories of the Other Side was the importance of getting that tooth removed. Gathering my strength, I made an appointment with my dentist and told him of the particular gold-crowned tooth in my mouth that needed to be pulled. He looked at the one in question and shook his head.

"Does it hurt?" he asked.

"No."

"It looks and seems okay," he said positively.

"It may look okay, but it has to come out," I replied emphatically.

He tried to reassure me that I was worrying needlessly. He took an X ray to appease me. As he showed it to me, he smiled and said, "Joyce, just as I thought, there is nothing wrong with this tooth." He showed me the X ray, carefully explaining why the tooth was sound.

But in my mind, I again saw the tooth: gold-crowned, suspended, rotating in front of me. Something was wrong with that tooth, and I knew it had to come out. To convince my dentist, I decided to share parts of my experience with him.

He listened carefully and politely, then shook his head slowly. "I'm sorry, Joyce. This experience you had just isn't enough for me."

He sighed, paused, and then continued, "Still, if you insist, I'll extract the tooth. But you'll need to sign a form releasing me from liability."

I readily agreed. He said he would make the

necessary arrangements, including the liability-release form, and suggested a later date for its removal. Disappointed because I was determined to have the tooth taken out immediately, I said, "I really want to get it out right away."

He clearly did not know what to make of my persistence. He shook his head again and then patiently told me, "If you feel it can't wait, the best I can do is refer you to a colleague."

He gave me the name of an oral surgeon. His receptionist called the oral surgeon's office and arranged an immediate appointment. My dentist let me take the X ray of my tooth to the appointment so that an additional one would not be required.

I explained to the oral surgeon that I wanted to keep the tooth after its removal. He anesthetized my mouth, extracted the tooth, and showed it to me.

As we examined the tooth, I was stunned. The roots were a peculiar darkened color, and even to my untrained eye it was obvious that they had deteriorated. They were oddly shaped and looked as if they had melted. The oral surgeon said very little as he examined the tooth while showing it to me. He placed it in a container for me and I left.

As I was leaving his office and for an hour

or two afterward, I felt strange sensations—as though thousands of electrical needles and pins were embedded in the skin all over my body and were working their way out to the surface through all of my pores. It was very uncomfortable. Within twenty-four hours, the mysterious bleeding down the back of my throat stopped as though a tap had been turned off. I was extremely grateful.

A few days after the extraction, I took the tooth back to my regular dentist on a follow-up visit, and he examined it closely. He asked if he could cut it in half to observe the interior. I agreed. Silver amalgam filling could be seen beneath the gold. (Until my experience on the Other Side, I didn't know about the severe health problems that could be caused by teeth *or* that silver amalgam or gold and silver in the same tooth could cause health problems.)

Within a few days, I went back to see the ear, nose, and throat specialist and took the gold-crowned tooth to show him. He held up half of it at a time with a pair of tweezers and examined it closely. He was usually a quiet man of few words who went in and out of the examination room briskly. Not this time. He looked from the roots of the tooth, to me, then back to the roots of the tooth. He exclaimed emphatically,

"Joyce, I never would have gotten you well with that in your mouth."

He told me the roots apparently had been embedded in the sinuses and had been "dissolved" by the infection. The infected tooth was the cause of the internal bleeding from my sinuses and had become too much for my system to overcome.

My delight at receiving that gift from God was soon joined by other blessings. Within two or three weeks the intense pain from my arthritis was almost completely gone. I had been given the chance to do all the things I wanted to do, to make this second chance at life the best gift from God possible.

Sharing the Truth

Shortly after my Other Side experience, I enthusiastically told several people close to me about it. However, I had mixed feelings about sharing it with anyone else—the subject wasn't openly discussed at that time. Also, this experience was sacred and personal to me.

And yet, I wanted to tell everyone what I had learned: Heavenly answers to earthly questions are available for all, and so is the knowledge that permits us to be certain of enjoying the Other Side when we get there. I remember wishing I could grab a megaphone and shout my message from the tallest building.

Eventually, I worked out a compromise. When another individual's need to hear about my experience on the Other Side became apparent, I shared it with assurance. At that time, I felt I was one of the most confident people on earth. I knew who I was: a child of God! For quite a while after my experience, I didn't think I'd ever fear being in the presence of other people again.

Gradually though, as time passed, my self-confidence in speaking about my experience began to dim. As I settled back into earth life, my experience and the lessons I had learned began to slip to the back of my mind rather than being the focus of my attention daily.

Answers in Action—How I Learned to Live the Lessons I Had Been Given

During the first few weeks after my return I was grateful for each problem awaiting me, because I knew of the benefits I could receive when I overcame them. By understanding problems in their proper, eternal perspective, I realized that each difficult experience, well lived with sincere intentions, was like a jewel in a crown. Its message would sparkle with rewards for having triumphed and passed through the refiner's fire.

With my new outlook at that time, I was able to see life's experiences in a different way. Trials were blessings, and I wanted to make it through them with the right attitude. The attitude I took in any given situation was my choice!

Realizing the rewards to be received by forgiving others, I wanted to forgive everyone for everything. I later wondered if I might have issued an unfortunate invitation for problems after my return to earth life.

Suspicions arose that my agents were working behind the scenes to cut me out of my twenty-year contract with a governmental entity. Finally, after tremendous efforts, my suspicions were confirmed. A new company had been created without my knowledge. My agents assigned my contract to this new, unknown company and listed it as its own asset in legal documents. Because of this breach in contract, the government contract was lost altogether. Everyone lost out on a project that could have benefited society and been profitable for all.

However, a substantial amount of money was owed me for my share of the project's earlier revenues. But in 1986, on the day I was to receive the check from my agents, I was told I would need an attorney to get it. I was devastated. On one hand, I wanted to forgive them, and move on. On the other hand . . . I needed that money. Reluctantly, I pursed legal action.

Staying on Track

Depressed because of this necessary action, I needed help to keep my thinking positive. I called upon all my past experiences and resources to design, create, and develop a more powerful Sleep Teaching course than any I had used before. It had positive suggestions to help me sleep, to help me handle the stress and to think and feel better.

Listening to those positive suggestions helped keep my thoughts and actions more in tune with the principles I had learned on the Other Side for a higher way of living. I used them continuously. Gradually I made it, hour by hour and day by day. This special course, with Super-Subliminals™ and Whisper Learning™, worked wonders.

Because the courses were unique and produced results, I had requests from people who wanted to purchase them and offers from others who wanted to market them. But I was trapped in a legal web and could not fill the requests at that time.

I believe that I would have won my lawsuit if I had had the needed strength and funds to keep fighting in the court system for the additional years that may have been required. However, more than six years of my life had already been consumed in this legal battle. Time was on the company's side to drag it out even longer.

The stress I was experiencing was almost unbearable. I had come to a point of depletion physically, financially, and emotionally. I realized that I had to close those painful chapters of my life, take my losses, forgive, forget, let go, and withdraw from the legal battle. I knew it would cost me my life to continue this fight any longer.

Then came another surprise, but this time a pleasant one—a settlement offer was made that would almost take care of the high costs and legal expenses I had accumulated. My prayers had not been answered as I had hoped, but I knew what truly mattered was to go on with my life the best I could.

When Is Losing Still Winning?

Drawing on the knowledge I gained when I was on the Other Side, I was extremely grateful to get through that very difficult period of time without becoming embittered. My prayers were answered with a peaceful feeling and with the assurance of rewards awaiting me on the Other Side instead of with "justice" or "victory" or material blessings here. As I continued to pray, my sorrow was swallowed up in the God-given inner peace that is available to all. I knew within my heart that I had passed a big test because I did not have any bad feelings toward those who had hurt me with their callous actions.

At that time, I saw things in the eternal perspective, and I felt sorrow for how much they were hurting themselves. I knew that God does not answer prayers by taking away others' free agency, and I couldn't blame God for the wrong choices others had made.

Because I knew I was exchanging my short allotment of time on earth for whatever I did that day, I was striving to look more carefully at my priorities. My time on earth is too short for me to remain angry or hold grudges against anyone; it is precious and limited when compared with the forever of eternity.

Making the Most of What Comes

Directly after my experience on the Other Side, with my new knowledge of the value of time, I thought that I would never again watch television or sit for hours in a movie theater. I did not want to waste one precious moment of my life. Now, however, I work at keeping a balance between worthwhile goals and needed leisure time; I do watch some television, but I am careful of quantity, content, and quality. I learned that the type and quality of music I listen to and of TV programs and movies I watch is worth carefully monitoring. I want the benefits of surrounding myself with inspirational and educational things rather than detrimental, destructive words or scenes.

Each hour of the day, I know that I make choices that include deliberately taking control of my thinking or allowing other forces to sway, dictate, or manipulate my thoughts and attitudes. I know that my attitudes and desires are formed as a direct result of the thoughts I hold daily in my mind, which then determine what I will accomplish during my life on earth.

Thoughts are powerful and too valuable to waste!

The Challenge of Living the Wisdom of the Other Side Here on Earth

A few years ago, I became aware of a business owned by a husband-and-wife team. They badly needed financial backing; they were on the brink of folding a business I believed had great potential. At a meeting one evening, they were discussing the way the business would be set up after they moved to a new location. The wife was bubbling with ideas; she wanted the employees to have half a day off each week to play golf. She also wanted them to have a lunchroom where classical music would play continually and elevate them to new levels of productivity.

Her husband wanted to have western music played in the lunchroom, and he emphatically made his viewpoint known. The debate was on. Voices began to rise. The couple was getting very angry over the type of music to be played in the lunchroom of a building that hadn't even been rented yet. The lunchroom never did materialize, nor did a system on which to play any music.

Now, whenever I find myself beginning to fuss over differing points of view, I pause, take a deep breath, and think, "Is this argument about music in the lunchroom?" Sometimes I laugh until tears roll down my cheeks as I stand back and see things from a better perspective.

It's amazing that people often get so involved in arguments that they could actually physically hurt each other over something similar to "music in the lunchroom." This experience reinforced the lessons I learned on the Other Side about the futility of arguing. I find it much easier now to let others express their opinions without contradicting them. It's not up to me to challenge the opinions of other people and try to get them to see things my way. I feel free from the need to defend my position—it's easier to compassionately listen and "let it go" if we disagree.

Letting Go of "Why Me?"

It was clear that I had wasted a lot of time before my experience on the Other Side thinking, "Why me? Why did this happen to me?"

Thoughts of "Why me?" or "Why now?" solve nothing and can lead to depression. Additionally, they waste valuable time and stop possible solutions that might otherwise come to mind. It would be as if my coat caught on fire and I yelled, "Why me?" as I wrung my hands while it burned rather than dousing the flames while they were still small. If I act, rather than ask "Why me?" I can put out the "fire" and be grateful it wasn't worse. Then I can practice "fire prevention" in the future. Handling problems in this manner helps me find solutions rather than waste time uselessly seeking answers that will not be revealed until I view things from the perspective of the Other Side.

On the Other Side, I became aware that there are many ways to handle problems in life. Running from them, though, or using drugs or drinking alcohol only makes them worse. Drugs and alcohol affect the chemicals in the brain and ultimately add to feeling depressed and overwhelmed—and can seriously damage health. They impair judgment and the ability to make decisions; the problems of those who use them increase and compound.

Drugs, alcohol, and negative thoughts can insidiously steal life because, under their influence, people are more apt to act impulsively on the false and deadly notion that suicide is a glamorous, or acceptable, way of escaping unwanted challenges. I was clearly shown that it is not!

Working with Problems, Not Around Them

Life presents problems, but working on them rather than hiding from them helps us find solutions. Ignoring problems or blaming others for them does not solve them. Facing them head-on, praying for strength and guidance to solve them and the wisdom to find their hidden benefits, reaps great rewards.

On the Other Side I had questioned, "What about those who died, found a beautiful, peaceful place, and came back to earth life again? Will they find that peace next time?" The answer was given me that it depends upon the intent of their hearts and their actions, as it does for all of us. My understanding was reinforced with the knowledge that we are required to endure whatever happens to us to the end of our lives.

As well as I know this, however, there are times when I find certain unwanted, familiar feelings starting to return, and I have to replace them with thoughts I know will help to create the actions and results I really want. Knowing that if I let my mind dwell on upsetting, unhappy thoughts, I will again attract "bad-habit thinking," I stop those thoughts by remembering what I experienced on the Other Side. The principles I learned there help me make it through difficult situations.

When I am feeling stressed or not feeling as mentally "up" as I would like, I usually call someone who I know needs help. I know it does not help to call someone to complain about life or to criticize. A technique I have found that works wonders is to call someone with cheerful good news or to help someone else have an "up" day. Helping someone else usually helps me.

Also, as I share my experience with others in a way that helps them, it helps me to relive it and remember what I learned from it. Remembering the significance and reality of what I experienced continues to help me here.

Does Talking About It Really Help?

As I described in the beginning of this book, I was first moved to speak out by the fear that others would be influenced by what they saw on that news program. For several years, my cousin Gloria, my mother, and several others urged me to publish my experiences, to reach a wider audience, but I hesitated. Then I began receiving letters and calls from people telling me of the positive differences my story had made in the lives of those with whom I had shared it; they wanted their own loved ones to know about it, too.

Ultimately, I gathered my courage and decided it was time to speak up more actively. Sometimes I speak on a one-to-one basis and other times with groups, as I feel prompted. Several times on an airplane the feeling has come to me that I must tell the person next to me a portion of my story.

When I get such feelings, they grow until I feel compelled to speak up. Then I begin a casual conversation and generally, with the other person's first few words, I learn why I felt impressed to speak to them. As I mentioned before, in many of life's situations, God uses people (whenever they are willing) to answer the prayers of others.

Since my return from the Other Side, there have been times that miraculous episodes have occurred when I told my story to strangers. Some needed a push to go to the dentist, others were suffering from an ailment that I accurately pinpointed, and they were then able to overcome it by seeking proper help.

Sometimes the person was feeling depressed or suicidal, and later I learned that he or she made life changes and was doing better. I was glad that our paths crossed when they did and that I was able to help.

The Gift Given Back

Upon returning to earth life, with the new, expanded knowledge I had gained, I felt more empathetic toward others. I treasure this empathy as a gift. When I look at the faces of other people now, whether I am speaking to an audience, seeing someone in a restaurant, sitting next to a stranger on an airplane or almost anywhere, I seem intuitively to discern the pain and joy that the people around me have experienced in their lives.

Sensing their inner beauty, struggles, and sincerity, or lack thereof, I begin to feel much about them. When I look into people's eyes and see their expressions, I understand them better and become aware of many of their needs, wants, fears, pains, and struggles.

I know we are progressing from one phase of history to another, from the past, through the present and into the future. I am extremely grateful that I was allowed to come back to earth and see some of these futuristic, remarkable things unfold. Having a better perspective helps me to understand more of what is taking place. It is fascinating to know that revolutionary technologies and marvelous inventions are coming, such as new, improved medical advances for maintaining health, outwitting disease, with faster, more accurate diagnostic techniques.

Some have already come about. It has been a marvelous experience to watch some of the things unfold that spark memories of being on the Other Side. Medical science has done almost unbelievable things, but there is yet much more to come, such as wondrous alternative-medicine cures, and other natural remedies and healing discoveries for the body.

The body is a truly miraculous gift of the Creator.

A Last Word on Prayer

Never think that no one is listening. Prayer is a special time, never to be underestimated.

After my experience on the Other Side, as I now pray, I picture God in my mind as a real, loving, personable, all-wise, all-powerful, and all-knowing God who wants me to be grateful for what I have.

As I kneel to pray in the morning, I feel it is helpful for me to take a few moments and call to mind those whom the Lord would have me be mindful of that day. By being more aware of others' needs, I feel more in tune with God. When I am more in harmony with His desired outcome of my day, I know I am more apt to have my prayers answered favorably and to receive His peace.

Also, I prefer to get in a reverent physical and spiritual setting when I can. I do not delay my prayers, though, just because I am not in the right place or I don't look right. He listens and can hear, no matter how or where someone prays to Him. His love is extended to all, regardless of situation and apparel. Prayers are answered according to His own timetable.

When I prepare myself before praying, I feel more respectful. God is as real as any other being—certainly more special than anyone I might meet in earth life. Just as I comb my hair

and straighten my appearance before opening
the door to a friend or stranger, I want to do so
before opening a dialogue with the most important being in my life. Prayer time can be anytime, anywhere, but I like to keep in mind with
whom I am conversing, and make it special
whenever I can.

My new attitude has to do with the reverence
and respect I feel for Him since I have come to
know Him better. In the Scripture that tells of
Moses approaching the burning bush, the voice
told him to remove his shoes, for the ground on
which he stood was holy. For me, now, I remind
myself that prayer time is holy time, and I want
to be even more respectful than I would talking
with any other person.

Usually, I want to tell Him how much I sincerely appreciate what I have been given, the
blessings I've received, and prayers that have
been answered. It is important to thank Him for
the gifts He has given before I ask for more.

It is not necessary to use eloquent speech
when I pray, because I know God is understanding and knows the intent of my heart. It is
important to pray in the manner I feel is comfortable and appropriate. When I was on the
Other Side, I learned that He wants to hear from

me—and from all of us. When I think of prayer as two-way communication, it becomes easier to pray.

What Keeps Me Going

There are moments when the veil seems to thin and memories from the Other Side return. These experiences are similar to walking into a room filled with dear and familiar people and experiences. Wondering how I could ever have forgotten some of them, I realize I didn't really forget. They are still there, but the pressures of day-to-day living pushed them to the back of my memory.

It is enjoyable when someone says something that refreshes my memory of scenes and feelings from the Other Side, and I recall how wondrously whole the purpose and plan of life really is. The combined feelings of love, connections to people, nature, knowledge about forgiveness and the desire to forgive others quickly well up within me. I re-experience some of the glorious feelings about life that I had then and deep gratitude for my mortal existence.

My love for others expanded when I learned the great eternal truth that each person is a unique individual with definite, differing personalities; that we always will be known by and unconditionally loved by God. Through whisperings of the Spirit, we can all know that we have always been uniquely us even before we were born. We didn't just begin with life on earth. We can also know that our identity continues after earth life—we don't stop being us at death.

From my experience on the Other Side, I learned many things. One conclusion I reached is that life is similar to a treasure chest filled with vast wonders, for here and for Heaven, but it has a big lock on it. Holding grudges, using harsh words, running from life and oneself by using drugs or alcohol and avoiding problems only makes the lock stronger.

There are "Grand Keys" to opening the lock that I learned. Among them are striving to be slow to anger, being quick to forgive, and seeking heavenly help by communicating with God through sincere prayer.

In addition, I know that problems can be solved by believing in miracles, expecting miracles, and helping to create miraculous results for someone else. All such miracles reap eternal rewards.

Giving Up Is Not an Option

With the new knowledge I had gained from being on the Other Side, my life changed. It was easier to live day to day. Not just from a health standpoint, but from an emotional one as well.

The challenges of pain and ill health are still factors in my life. Yet they are immaterial when my perspective is clear. I gladly accept my body and its health problems. Whether I am slender or not is no longer a big issue for me. It is my body, good or bad, and I'm grateful for it. I do not know what the future holds, but I am very grateful for each day.

As I write this, I am reminded of a message I put on a wall plaque. It is from the poem "Salutation to the Dawn," author unknown. I adapted and added to this saying, and sometimes I give it out at speaking engagements:

Yesterday is already a dream, tomorrow is
    only a vision;
but today, well lived, makes every yesterday
    a dream of happiness,
and every tomorrow a vision of hope.
Celebrate Life. This Is Not a Dress Rehearsal!

The Need for Help Rather than Advice

Before my near-death experience in 1983, I had tried many different things through the years to help myself, but feelings of depression and thoughts of suicide continued to creep into my mind. Their alluring appeal was based on false notions of escaping from life's problems and gaining unearned peace.

Friends and family offered such advice as "Get hold of yourself," and "Pull yourself together! How can you be blue when you have so many blessings?" and "Snap out of it!" When I was depressed to the point of considering suicide and I would hear, "Think of your family," it only made me feel more suicidal because I wrongly felt they were selfish to ask me to live when I wanted to die.

I would caution those approached by people who are voicing thoughts of suicide. Statements that may seem like good advice are usually not well received by someone feeling downhearted and overwhelmed. The "Get hold of yourself" types of comments do not help but rather add to their feelings of hopelessness and inadequacy, and in fact can make them feel worse and even push them deeper into depression.

If it were always possible for people who feel

extremely depressed to pull themselves together and get on with their lives, there would be few people with depression. It's important to realize that when people feel depressed for an extended period of time they may no longer be able to pull their mood up by themselves. They need help!

There are ways to help the suicidal person realize his or her own life's value. Everyone involved needs to seek help.

Take Control and Fight for Life

If you are the one feeling depressed, listen to your feelings and the whisperings of the Spirit. Seek help actively! Ask for it. Don't be put off. Go to a doctor, a religious leader, a counselor. Fight for life. Pray and pray again! We are each responsible for our own happiness. Taking control of our thoughts, feelings, attitudes, and consequently our lives often means seeking out the best resources we can find to help us solve our particular problems. I have discovered that I must be a detective, searching out ideas and resources to make life as full as I can for myself in caring for my mind, body, and spirit. I know that I must be aware of my moods and continually remind myself of my true purpose for living and of the true, lasting peace of mind to be found in right thinking.

I feel I must warn as many people as possible, any who will listen to what I discovered: We are our own judges! When we get to the Other Side too soon and realize what we gave up and the sorrow or pain we caused others, we may experience emotional torture of our own making that is true agony.

The Great Benefits of Hanging On

There are times in life when you may be faced with the choice of giving up on life or going on. Please hear my message. Life is worth living!

Choosing otherwise can steal away great joys. It is not a chance worth taking. I learned that life offers rich opportunities even in seeming defeats. Glorious rewards can be earned and enjoyed in this life, and especially on the Other Side, with right thoughts, actions, and kind deeds.

Circumstances are constantly changing—often for the better. At least during earth life we can still repent, find solutions, and grow wiser. Death is so final. Suicidal thoughts are false, futile attempts to escape from problems rather than solve them. They short-circuit thinking and add to problems and feelings of depression. Suicidal thoughts always contain life-threatening myths!

Suicidal thoughts actually stopped me from finding solutions.

The anguish from my wrong actions created an unquenchable burning and searing of my conscience. It was agonizing to realize I had lost great rewards of happiness as a result of my choices, when enduring and hanging on a little longer could have brought me the rewards of eternal victory with my family and loved ones.

Again, only God knows the full answers to questions regarding those who commit suicide, and only He can administer a fair judgment and decide the degree of each person's accountability. Even though individuals may feel depressed and miserable in life, they *may* feel enormously worse on the Other Side if they kill themselves.

God's Greatest Gift

During my near-death experience, I learned that life is God's greatest gift to each of us. To throw it away by committing suicide is possibly one of the worst acts one can commit—it is offensive and disrespectful to Him. Suicide is a tragedy for all concerned.

Also, I learned that when people have sincerely tried to meet their challenges and it is their time to die, they can pass on to a welcoming home from those who love them on the Other Side and enjoy the fruits of their labors on earth. They can look forward to the harvest of good deeds and good attitudes by having endured well to the end. Such individuals will be met by heavenly family, friends, angels, and God with mutual rejoicing over earthly achievements.

PART FOUR

❦

Highlights from Heaven:
An Overview

My experience was the most realistic event of my life. While I was on the Other Side all of my senses were expanded beyond anything possible in mortal life. By comparison, earth life is the dream world. Realism is found only on the Other Side.

Taking just one example, that of knowledge—never during earth life could my mind have grasped what it did there. It was as if I were drinking from some vast pool of forgotten wisdom. Information poured into me the instant I formulated a question. And much of what I knew over there seemed to come from within me, as if from a dormant pool that had suddenly become energized in this different sphere.

It was a different sphere—one in which knowledge was readily available to the earnest seeker and one in which the concept of time was meaningless. The past, present, and future seemed accessible on demand. And the place was permeated with love—love that rises to emotional heights undreamed of in earthly terms.

Another great truth that I learned while I was on the Other Side is that enduring well while making it through problems in earth life will bring such great satisfaction and peace of mind over there that it defies description. It is like discovering that there is a great retirement fund in Heaven which is built by overcoming problems during earth life with loving, forgiving, and charitable attitudes and actions. Such actions create heavenly rewards that include eternal peace and joy.

Not all of what I saw was pleasant, of course, and this added to the realism of the experience. Those I saw who had committed suicide, for example, were pitiful creatures who had somehow broken a premortal promise to make the most of their lives. Their agony of missed opportunity was clearly evident; I shared some of their feelings because I had willed myself to die.

Life's events, good and bad, were put into an

eternal perspective that finally made sense to me. Never, with the dim earthly understanding that I had before my experience, could I have fathomed the meaning and purposes of life as I did there. I came to understand that earthly life is a gift precious beyond belief.

My return to life was a wondrous, welcome reprieve. My choice to return was driven by my desire to remedy my approach to life and its problems. With my new understanding of what I could have been, life, with all of its trials and challenges, became an exciting adventure with almost limitless opportunities. If I dealt successfully with those opportunities, then a boundless future awaited me—an expansive future, in a marvelous, glorious sphere, limited only by my own thoughts and actions.

Other events after my return gave further evidence of the reality of my experience. The healing I enjoyed after my horribly debilitating illness, although not complete, was sufficient to allow me to realize my newfound life's mission. This healing defied most medical wisdom of the time. My recognition of the devastation created by my infected tooth was unexplainable by the best medical help I could get at the time. Yet the tooth's removal proved the efficacy of my Other Side's vision.

My experience was the essence of reality. Purposely, I believe, my memory has dimmed some of the things I knew with such clarity on the Other Side; still, the vision of that wondrous place is vivid in my mind. It will always be so. When flashes of memory bring back some of the feelings I had there, I experience a longing or homesickness for what I know to be my real home. Fortunately, these feelings evolve into a desire to live this life to the fullest—to measure up to my full stature as a daughter of God. Someday, from the Other Side, I will look back at my actions in this life. Then I want to know that I lived up to my premortal promises and fulfilled my mission in life and my purpose for living.

The following are some of the most vivid impressions I received from my Other Side experience:

Sincere Givers Gain

As we give, so shall we receive:
When we give criticism,
we receive criticism.

When we are hostile,
we cause fighting.

When we ridicule,
we receive ridicule and
become shy.

When we are tolerant,
we learn to be patient.

When we give praise,
we learn to appreciate others and
we receive appreciation.

When we are fair,
we are more apt to receive
justice.

When we have faith,
we receive security.

When we give approval,
we receive love.

When we give friendship, acceptance, and
unconditional love, we find
peace and love in the world. . . . Sincere Givers gain.

JOYCE H. BROWN

I pray that this book will be an influence for good to those who feel overwhelmed and stressed by life and to those who mistakenly long for the peace of death. I especially pray that it will restrain those who may be contemplating ending their own lives.

As I ponder my experiences on the Other Side, my outstanding impressions are of the importance of being forgiving, of unconditionally loving others, and of not judging, criticizing, nor complaining.

I remember vividly the impression of the absolute, all-encompassing LOVE that radiated, permeated, and engulfed me while I was in the presence of that all-powerful Being of Love and Light where I learned heavenly answers to earthly questions.

SIGNET

Brad Steiger and Sherry Hansen Steiger

❑ CHILDREN OF THE LIGHT

0-451-18533-1/$4.99

❑ HEAVEN IS OUR HOME

0-451-19777-1/$5.99

❑ MOTHER MARY SPEAKS TO US

0-451-18804-7/$5.99

Brad Steiger

❑ GUARDIAN ANGELS AND SPIRIT GUIDES

0-451-19544-2/$5.99

❑ HE WALKS WITH ME

0-451-19213-3/$5.99

❑ ONE WITH THE LIGHT

0-451-18415-7/$4.99

❑ RETURNING FROM THE LIGHT

0-451-18623-0/$5.99